Power Analysis and Trend Detection for Water Quality Monitoring Data

An Application for the Greater Yellowstone Inventory and Monitoring Network

Natural Resource Report NPS/GRYN/NRR—2012/556

Kathryn M. Irvine

Statistician
U.S. Geological Survey
Rocky Mountain Science Center
Bozeman, MT 59715

Kezia Manlove, Cynthia Hollimon

Department of Mathematical Sciences
Montana State University
Bozeman, MT 59715

July 2012

U.S. Department of the Interior
National Park Service
Natural Resource Program Center
Fort Collins, Colorado

The National Park Service, Natural Resource Stewardship and Science office in Fort Collins, Colorado publishes a range of reports that address natural resource topics of interest and applicability to a broad audience in the National Park Service and others in natural resource management, including scientists, conservation and environmental constituencies, and the public.

The Natural Resource Report Series is used to disseminate high-priority, current natural resource management information with managerial application. The series targets a general, diverse audience, and may contain NPS policy considerations or address sensitive issues of management applicability.

All manuscripts in the series receive the appropriate level of peer review to ensure that the information is scientifically credible, technically accurate, appropriately written for the intended audience, and designed and published in a professional manner.

This report received formal peer review by subject-matter experts who were not directly involved in the collection, analysis, or reporting of the data, and whose background and expertise put them on par technically and scientifically with the authors of the information.

Views, statements, findings, conclusions, recommendations, and data in this report do not necessarily reflect views and policies of the National Park Service, U.S. Department of the Interior. Mention of trade names or commercial products does not constitute endorsement or recommendation for use by the U.S. Government.

This report is available from the Greater Yellowstone Network website (http://science.nature.nps.gov/im/units/gryn/), the Integration of Natural Resource Management Applications website (https://irma.nps.gov/), and the Natural Resource Publications Management website (http://www.nature.nps.gov/publications/nrpm/).

Please cite this publication as:

Irvine, K. M., K. Manlove, and C. Hollimon. 2012. Power analysis and trend detection for water quality monitoring data: An application for the Greater Yellowstone Inventory and Monitoring Network. Natural Resource Report NPS/GRYN/NRR—2012/556. National Park Service, Fort Collins, Colorado.

NPS 960/115849, July 2012

Contents

Contents (continued)

Figures

Figures (continued)

Tables

Abstract

An important consideration for long term monitoring programs is determining the required sampling effort to detect trends in specific ecological indicators of interest. To enhance the Greater Yellowstone Inventory and Monitoring Network's water resources protocol(s) (O'Ney 2006 and O'Ney et al. 2009 [under review]), we developed a set of tools to: (1) determine the statistical power for detecting trends of varying magnitude in a specified water quality parameter over different lengths of sampling (years) and different within-year collection frequencies (monthly or seasonal sampling) at particular locations using historical data, and (2) perform periodic trend analyses for water quality parameters while addressing seasonality and flow weighting.

A power analysis for trend detection is a statistical procedure used to estimate the probability of rejecting the hypothesis of no trend when in fact there is a trend, within a specific modeling framework. In this report, we base our power estimates on using the seasonal Kendall test (Helsel and Hirsch 2002) for detecting trend in water quality parameters measured at fixed locations over multiple years. We also present procedures (R-scripts) for conducting a periodic trend analysis using the seasonal Kendall test with and without flow adjustment. This report provides the R-scripts developed for power and trend analysis, tutorials, and the associated tables and graphs. The purpose of this report is to provide practical information for monitoring network staff on how to use these statistical tools for water quality monitoring data sets.

Acknowledgments

We thank Cathie Jean and Sue O'Ney for their initiation and guidance of this project. We also thank Jeff Arnold, Cassity Bromley, Adam Sigler, and the numerous field technicians who have helped to implement the network water resources monitoring program over the years, and Rob Daley for his assistance with data preparation and delivery for this project. We sincerely thank both Jeff Warren (USFWS) and David Thoma (NPS) for reviewing this document and providing comments that enhanced our presentation of the methods. K.M. Irvine, C. Hollimon, and K. Manlove's participation was made possible through a CESU agreement with the Department of Mathematical Sciences at Montana State University (RM-CESU Cooperative Agreement Number: H1200090004 and J2120100010). Any use of trade, firm, or product names is for descriptive purposes only and does not imply endorsement by the U.S. Government.

Introduction

In 2001, the National Park Service (NPS) initiated a long-term ecological monitoring program, called the Vital Signs Monitoring Program, to monitor targeted physical, chemical, and biological indicators of park "health" over time and space (Fancy et al. 2008). The selected suite of ecological indicators are referred to collectively as "vital signs." Across the United States the national parks have been organized into networks of park units under the umbrella of the Vital Signs Monitoring Program. An important consideration for long term monitoring programs is determining the required sampling effort to detect trends in specific ecological indicators of interest. Commonly, this assessment is based on a statistical power analysis in combination with logistical and budget constraints. The Greater Yellowstone Network (GRYN) supports vital signs monitoring in Bighorn Canyon National Recreation Area (NRA) and Grand Teton and Yellowstone national parks (NP). Here we describe tools developed for the GRYN water resources vital sign.

During the vital signs selection process, the GRYN, along with the parks and specialists, identified water resources as one of its vital signs for long-term monitoring (Jean et al. 2005). In 2005, the network initiated monitoring water bodies identified by the states of Montana and Wyoming as "water quality impaired" which are state 303(d)/305(b) listed rivers and streams. The GRYN capitalized on monitoring efforts from previous years. By 2009, monitoring activities had been expanded to include water quality of impaired waters in Bighorn Canyon NRA and Yellowstone NP, outstanding natural resource waters in Grand Teton NP and Yellowstone NP, high alpine lakes in Grand Teton NP, and non-listed or impaired perennial streams and springs in Bighorn Canyon NRA. Also in 2009, the monitoring protocol was revised (O'Ney et al. 2009 [under review]) to combine the regulatory protocol (O'Ney 2006)—aimed at monitoring state 303(d)/305(b) listed rivers and streams with the network's other water resource monitoring needs. This expanded protocol (O'Ney et al. 2009 [under review]) can be found at http://science.nature.nps.gov/im/monitor/VitalSigns/BrowseProtocol.aspx. Since 2009, the network and parks reevaluated the water resources monitoring program and reduced the number of sample sites in order to maintain an effective program within logistical and budget constraints. The tools described in this paper helped with that decision making process and will continue to be used during further refinement of the protocol.

In Chapter 1, we describe our procedure to estimate the power for trend detection of the seasonal Kendall test. Water quality parameters are notorious for their skewness and non-normal error distributions. Therefore, one of the most commonly used trend tests in water resources is the seasonal Kendall test, a non-parametric approach for monotonic trend detection at specific sites (locations) that accommodates seasonality (Helsel and Hirsch 2002). We developed an empirical bootstrap approach to estimate the power for trend detection of the seasonal Kendall test to avoid requiring any distributional assumptions. This approach is suitable for programs that have long-term datasets that are available and representative of the variation and skewness of water quality parameters at a given location. Our procedure allows for conducting a power analysis for detecting monotonic trends of varying magnitude over different lengths of sampling and different collection frequencies at particular sampling locations. In Chapter 2, we present a description of the functions we have created to perform the seasonal Kendall test with and without flow adjustment.

Throughout this document we use data from the GRYN as a motivating example. The R-scripts and quick reference tutorials on the use of the R scripts are provided as appendices.

Chapter 1. Power Analysis

A power analysis for trend is a statistical procedure used to estimate the probability of rejecting the hypothesis of no trend when in fact there is a trend (making the right decision), within a specific modeling framework. Statistical power can be increased by increasing sample size (in the case of site-specific trends, the number of years of data collection). Power can also be increased by reducing the variation (noise) in the data by flow adjustment or improved quality assurance/quality control (QA/QC) procedures. Other factors that contribute to statistical power include the specific effect size of interest (later referred to as γ; the larger the effect, the greater the power to detect that effect) and the probability of Type 1 error (α) (lower αs yield lower power). The probability of Type 1 error is the probability of detecting a trend when in fact there is not one. All of these factors interact. Through iteration of the power analysis code, one is able to determine the various combinations of the number of years, within-year sampling frequency, and effect size that lead to a given power desired for a given parameter at a given location. Others have pointed out the importance of considering the trade-offs between Type I and Type II error rates (Buhl-Mortensen 1996, Gibbs et al. 1998, Mapstone 1995) when designing long-term monitoring protocols.

In this example, we use the seasonal Kendall test (Helsel and Hirsch 2002) to detect trends in water quality parameters measured at fixed locations over time. We use the seasonal Kendall test because we expect the data to exhibit some seasonality in at least a few of the parameters (that is, we expect median parameter values to differ from season to season), as opposed to the conventional Kendall's tau, τ, which does not account for seasonality within the data. The R-code provided in Appendix B can be used to find the power of detecting a non-zero trend in a water quality parameter of interest (e.g., temperature) given data collection within pre-determined hydrologic seasons or months within each year, a certain number of years of data collection, a given annual multiplicative change in the water quality parameter (e.g., a 2.5% annual increase in median temperature over 10 years), and a specified α-level. The reliability of the power estimates, however, is dependent on the assumption that the variability in the data used in the R-code is representative of current or future conditions.

As a demonstration of our approach we use data collected from the Snake River Yellowstone National Park (YELL) location. We provide the estimated power to detect a 2.5% annual change in dissolved oxygen (DO), temperature, conductivity, and pH at the Snake River YELL location (Figure 1.1). This rate of change was chosen arbitrarily based on graphically displaying the simulated data under the alternative. Water quality experts should be consulted to determine if these scenarios are biologically plausible and of interest.

Data preparation is discussed in the following section and additional information is provided in Appendix A. The R-code to run the procedure is provided in Appendix B. Within the code the following user inputs are required: the magnitude of annual multiplicative change of interest, the number of years for sampling (e.g., 10, 20, 30 years), probability of Type I error (α), the assumed seasons based on the hydrograph (the options are "YELL" for Yellowstone National Park locations, "BICA" for Bighorn Canyon National Recreational Area locations, or "GRTE" for Grand Teton National Park), the water quality parameters of interest (e.g., temperature, DO, pH, conductance), the number of seasons within a year based on cumulative hydrograph analysis (e.g., 3, 4 or 12), and whether or not to conduct a comparison of collecting data once per hydrograph season or once a month (T to compare, F otherwise). A step-by-step guide to running the R-code is available in Appendix C.

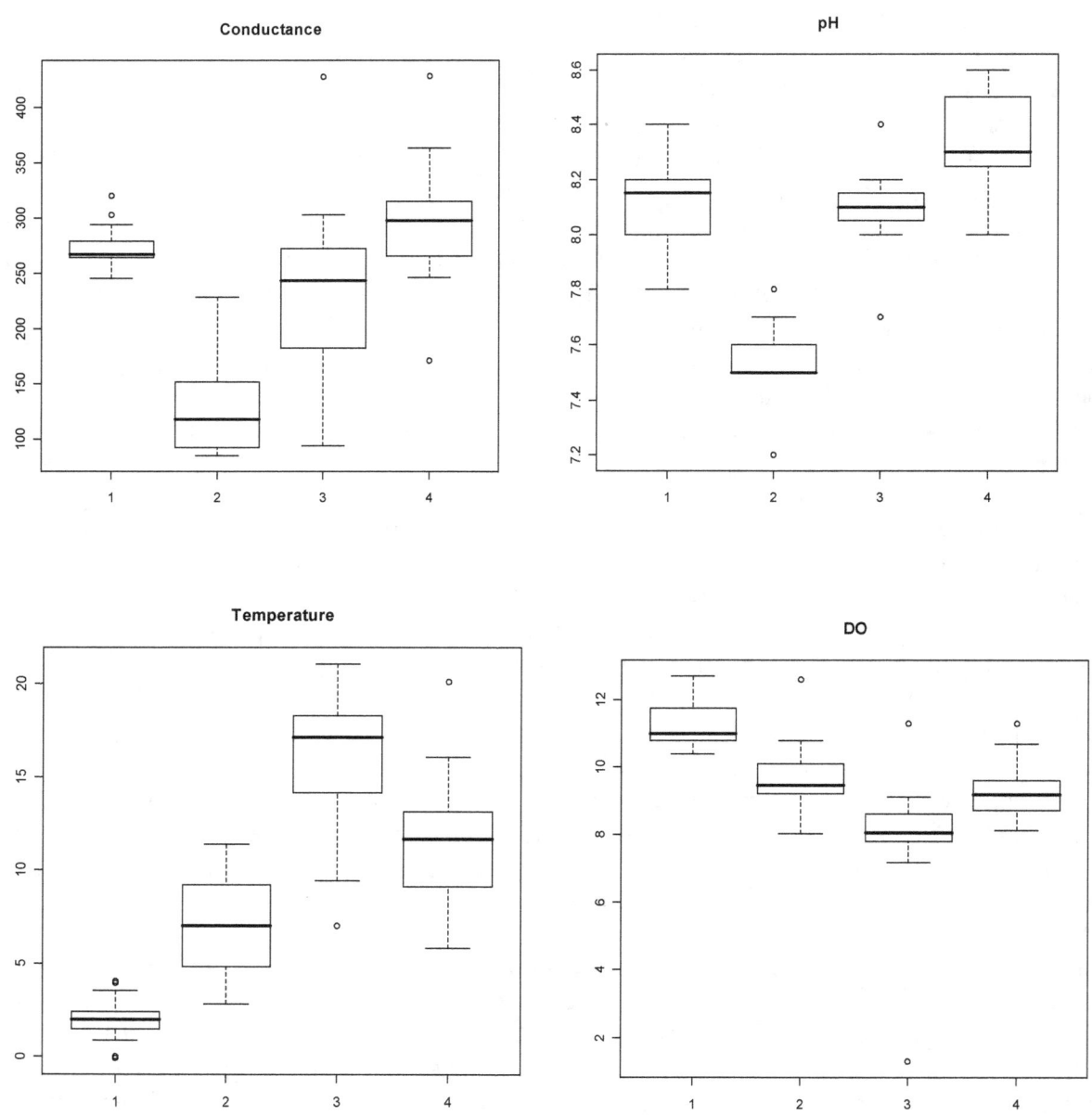

Figure 1.1. Available pilot data at the Snake River YELL location since 2002 for the four water quality parameters: conductance, temperature, pH, and dissolved oxygen (DO) by season.

Data Considerations

Data were collected throughout the GRYN from the mid-1960s to current. For this investigation we used only the data since 2002 because the QA/QC procedures were improved during this time period compared to the "historic" data. We make the assumption that these data are more representative of data to be collected at present and into the future at these specific locations. This assumption can not be understated, the power estimates are only reliable if there is enough pre-exisiting data to characterize the variation and skewness within a season or a month over years.

The hydrologic definition of seasons used in the R-code for the three parks are in Table 1.1. The user specifies which park the stream data correspond to (YELL, BICA, or GRTE) and the season is defined accordingly within the R code. We assume that one observation will be available per season for every year of sampling. We do not consider missing observations that may arise due to inability to access locations or equipment failure nor do we consider nondetections. The R-code also allows for calculating the estimated power assuming data are collected once per month.

Table 1.1. Hydrologic definition of seasons for the three parks within the GRYN.

	BICA	YELL	GRTE
1	August 10-April 14	November 1-April 15	August 15-April 14
2	April 15-June 19	April 16-June 15	April 15-June 9
3	June 20-August 9	June 16-August 15	June 10-August 14
4		August 16-October 31	

We suggest the user summarize their pilot data using boxplots as in Figure 1.1. Boxplot summaries provide an indication of the median horizontal midline of box, 25th [lower end of box] and 75th percentile values [upper end of box], the whiskers extend to the most extreme data points that are within 1.5 times the interquartile range, and circles represent data points outside of the whiskers [outliers]. This step should be done prior to running the R-code provided in this document to verify the input data set is representative of current and future variation and that there are no obvious errors in the data. The following R code can be used to create the plots, `boxplot(pH~Season, varwidth=T)`, the width of the boxes will be proportional to sample size.

Outline of Power Analysis Procedure

The first steps of this power analysis procedure are to determine a given level of annual trend (γ_A) that is scientifically meaningful to use as an alternative hypothesis, the number of years for sampling, and the desired Type 1 error rate (the probability of detecting a trend when in fact there is not one). In order to estimate power, we use a Monte Carlo procedure to estimate power using the following steps:

1. The pilot data are de-seasonalized to yield a set of season residuals ($\varepsilon*$). The season-specific median value is subtracted from each observation. If the monthly option is chosen, the corresponding monthly median is subtracted from each observation.

2. Simulate values of the response of interest with a given magnitude of trend over time for a given number of years. The $\varepsilon*$s derived from the pilot data are used to add a

stochastic component to the simulated data that is representative of the inherent variability and skewness of the water quality parameter within seasons or months.

3. Compute the seasonal Kendall's tau correlation coefficient (S) for the simulated data.

4. Test if S is significant and record outcome.

5. Repeat steps 3 and 4 between 500 and 1000 iterations. Count the number of times that the null hypothesis of no trend in the data is rejected.

6. The estimate of statistical power for the seasonal Kendall test is determined for a given magnitude of change over a given number of years by dividing the number of times that the null hypothesis is rejected in step 5 by the total number of iterations conducted (the number of bootstrap replications), conditional on a specified α level for the test.

Each step of the procedural outline is expounded upon below assuming the seasonal option for sampling. If monthly sampling were assumed, the R-code specifies 12 seasons (i.e., months).

Step 1: Determining γ-values of interest

In the model, γ governs how quickly the seasonal median response changes annually. Very high values of γ correspond to rapid changes, whereas smaller values indicate more gradual change over time. $\gamma=0$ corresponds to no change in the median over time. In the example, we set the annual rate of change in the median to be 2.5%. Figure 1.2 and 1.3 display one realization of data (simulated data) under this assumed rate of change for the four parameters at the Snake River YELL location. Notice there are four lines, one for each season across many years All lines display a common trend, but the intercepts are different based on the estimated median for each season. This type of graphical display (Figure 1.2 and Figure 1.3) can be used to assess whether the user defined levels of change and input pilot data produce biologically realistic patterns of variation and trends over years.

Step 2: Obtaining ε*s from the pilot data

We used the pilot data to obtain values for the seasonal residuals (ε^*) by subtracting the median for each season from the observed water quality parameter values. To be conservative, we assume that the variability and propensity for extreme observations are season specific. For example, Figure 1.4 displays the residuals for conductance at Snake River YELL location; there is an obvious difference in terms of variability and outliers across the four seasons. This pattern suggests that re-sampling residuals within season is the most appropriate bootstrap approach to use compared to an approach that resamples residuals across all seasons.

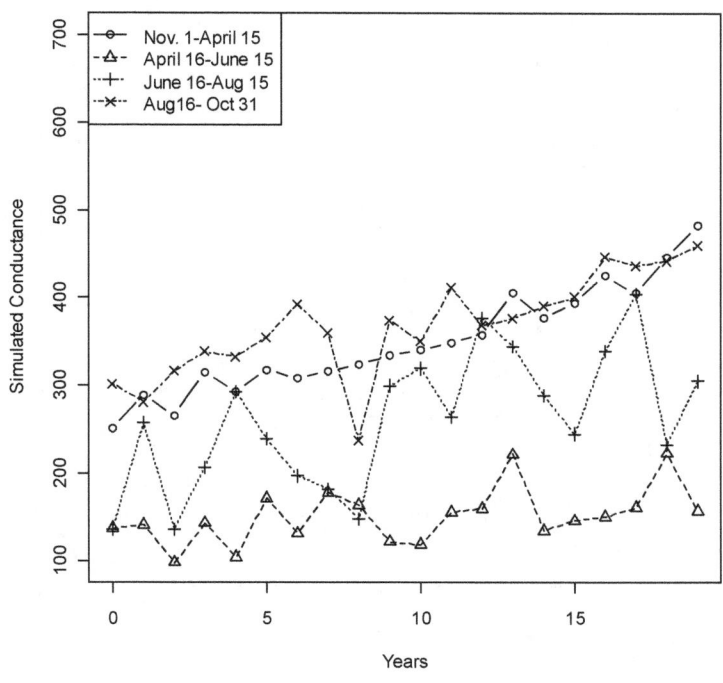

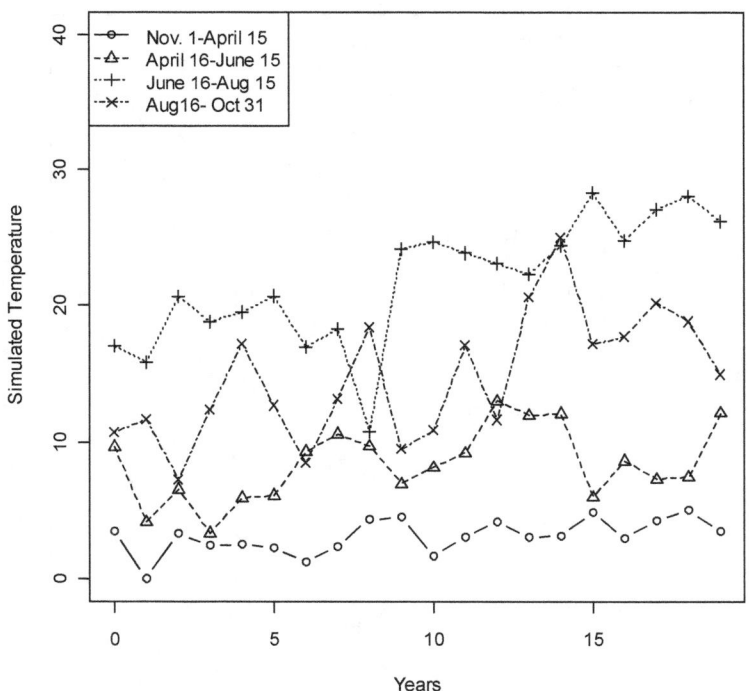

Figure 1.2. Simulated data for conductiance and temperature assuming a 2.5% annual change in the median for each of four hydrograph seasons over 20 years using data from the Snake River at YELL location.

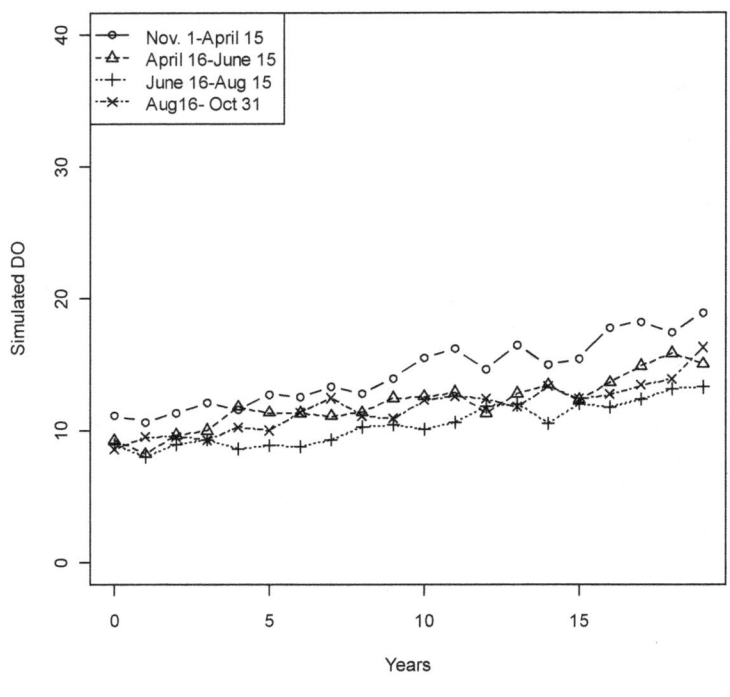

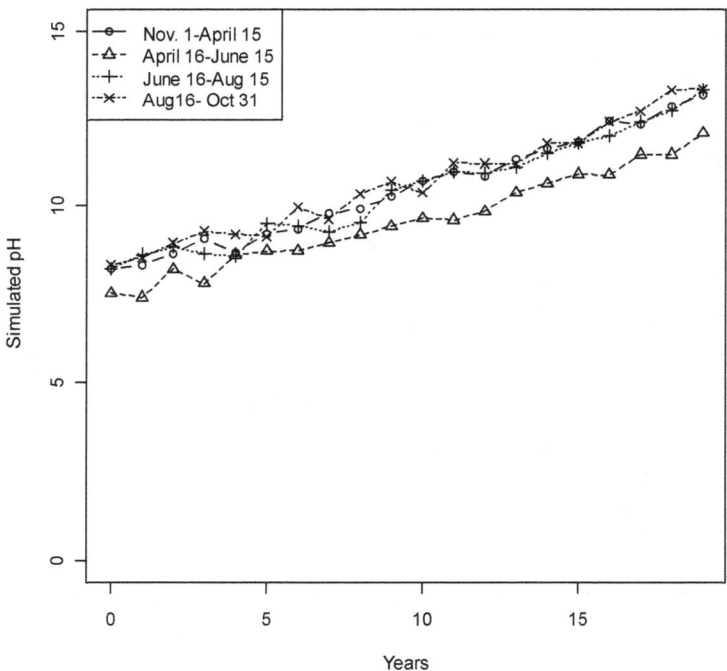

Figure 1.3. Simulated data for DO and pH assuming a 2.5% annual change in the median for each of four hydrograph seasons over 20 years using data from the Snake River at YELL location.

18

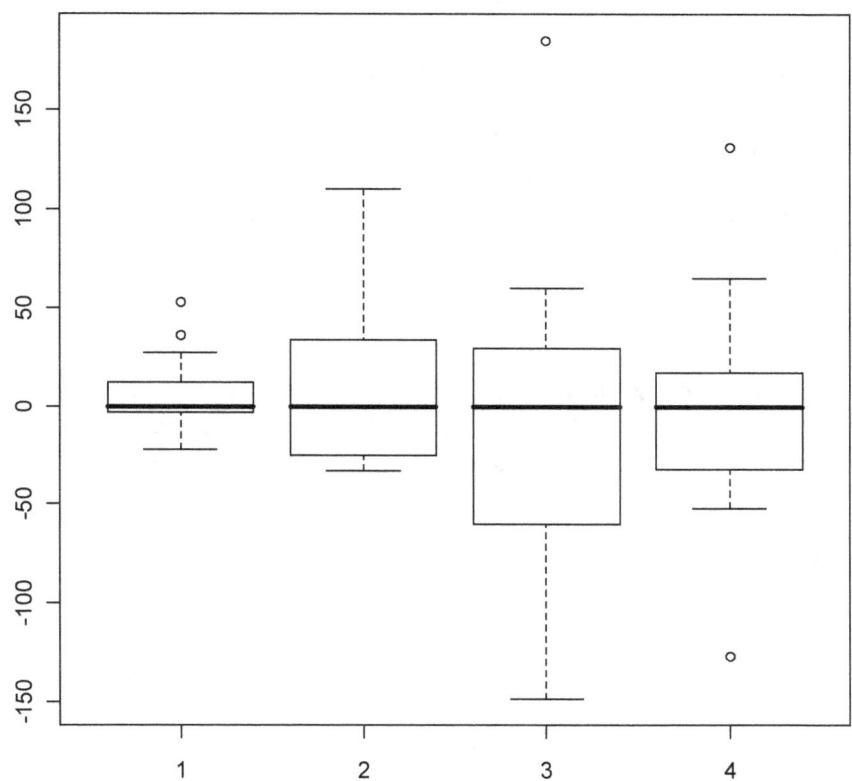

Figure 1.4. Boxplot of residuals by season for water conductance at the Snake River Yellowstone National Park location (only used data collected since 2002).

Step 3: Simulating values of the response with trend (under the alternative hypothesis)
To simulate data over years under a given annual rate of change we extended the model proposed in Yue and Pilon (2004) to multiple seasons. We simulated data under the monotonic non-linear model expressed as:

$$Y_{ij} = b_j \exp(\gamma \times Year_i) + \varepsilon_{ij}, \qquad (1)$$

where Y_{ij} is the data value in the ith year and j^{th} season, γ is the multiplicative annual rate of change, b_j is the median for season j estimated from the pilot data, Year is the integer value representing the ith year (e.g., 0,1,2,…,), and ε_{ij} is a randomly selected residual from the appropriate seasonal ε^* distribution. The model in Equation 1 specifies that the trend is a fixed multiplicative increase in the seasonal median plus the stochastic error (ε_{ij}). This simulation procedure produces a set of data with a specified multiplicative trend over time.

Figure 1.2 and 1.3 display an example of data simulated under this model with $\gamma = 0.025$. For example the simulated Conductance variable in Figure 1.2 (top panel) is a combination of the deterministic portion of Equation 1, specifically the median in the hydrograph season corresponding to November 1-April 15 is ~250 in year 0 by year 30 the median is essentially

19

doubled (250*exp(.025*29)=516). The stochastic variation around this median value is induced from the bootstrap error distribution. We see that in Figure 1.3 the variation in the residuals in season 1 is quite low, so the simulated value in year 20 is very close to this median value. There is very little variation in the seasonal trend line for November 1 to April 15 compared to the other seasons with more variation in the empirical residuals.

Our empirical bootstrap approach retains the outliers in the pilot dataset by using a re-sampling procedure from that empirical distribution as opposed to assuming the residuals ε_{ij} follow a parametric distribution (e.g., Gaussian). Assumptions in the data simulation procedure include 1) that the yearly trend is monotonically increasing without bounds, 2) the trend is assumed to be the same across seasons, 3) the errors are additive, and 4) an observation is recorded for each season and year (no missing values or non-detections).

Step 4: Computing seasonal Kendall's Tau (S) for a given alternative hypothesis
After the data are simulated, we calculated Kendall's τ within each season (Hirsch et al. 1982, Kendall 1975). Let S_j be the value of Kendall's τ for season j, where j ϵ {1, 2, ..., J}. Then

$$S_j = \sum_{k=1}^{n_j-1} \sum_{l=k+1}^{n_j} sign(y_{lj} - y_{kj}),$$

where

$$sign(y_{lj} - y_{kj}) = \begin{cases} 1 & y_{lj} - y_{kj} > 0 \\ 0 & y_{lj} - y_{kj} = 0 \\ -1 & y_{lj} - y_{kj} < 0 \end{cases}.$$

That is, Kendall's τ for season j is the sum of the signs of the differences between values of every pair of successive measurements/simulations of a variable within season j.

We used seasonal Kendall's τ (S), which is the sum of all the within-season estimates of

$$S = \sum_{j=1}^{J} S_j$$

Kendall's τ (S_j) for each simulation, $\quad$ (J =3 or 4). The test statistic for a given simulated dataset is calculated by

$$Z_S = \begin{cases} \dfrac{S-1}{\sqrt{var(S)}} & S > 0 \\ 0 & S = 0 \\ \dfrac{S+1}{\sqrt{var(S)}} & S < 0 \end{cases},$$

$$\sigma_S = \sum_{j=1}^{J} \sqrt{\frac{n_j(n_j-1)(2n_j-5)}{18}}$$

where $\quad$ (Hirsch et al. 1982). We calculate the variance assuming there are no ties in the data, likely true for the simulated data with trend. The variance will

20

decrease if there are ties (see Helsel and Hirsch 2002:215-216 for the correction to the variance term in the presence of ties).

Step 5: Testing significance of seasonal Kendall's Tau, S

A significance test for trend accounting for differences in seasonal medians can be performed by comparing Z_S to a critical value ($z_{\alpha/2}$), which is the value that has a probability of greater than $\alpha/2$ under the standard normal distribution (Hirsch et al. 1982). For one iteration, we record 0 if $|Z_S| <$ $z_{\alpha/2}$ and 1 otherwise.

It should be noted that $Z_S \rightarrow Z$ asymptotically, thus the standard normal distribution's capacity to truly reflect the population from which our data arise will diminish for $n_j < 10$ (Helsel and Hirsch 2002), where n_j is the number of years for season j. Power estimates are possibly unstable if the user specifies less than 10 years of sampling. However, we tested using the Snake River at YELL pilot data whether the nominal error rate (observed power when data is simulated with no trend in seasonal medians over years) is effected and it did not appear to differ as a function of number of years of sampling (Figure 1.5). This is reassuring that the procedure should provide a representative estimate of the power to detect trend using the seasonal Kendall test. However, there are bootstrap or exact approaches available for hypothesis testing in the cases of small sample sizes (less than 10 years of data) that are described in the R package Kendall.

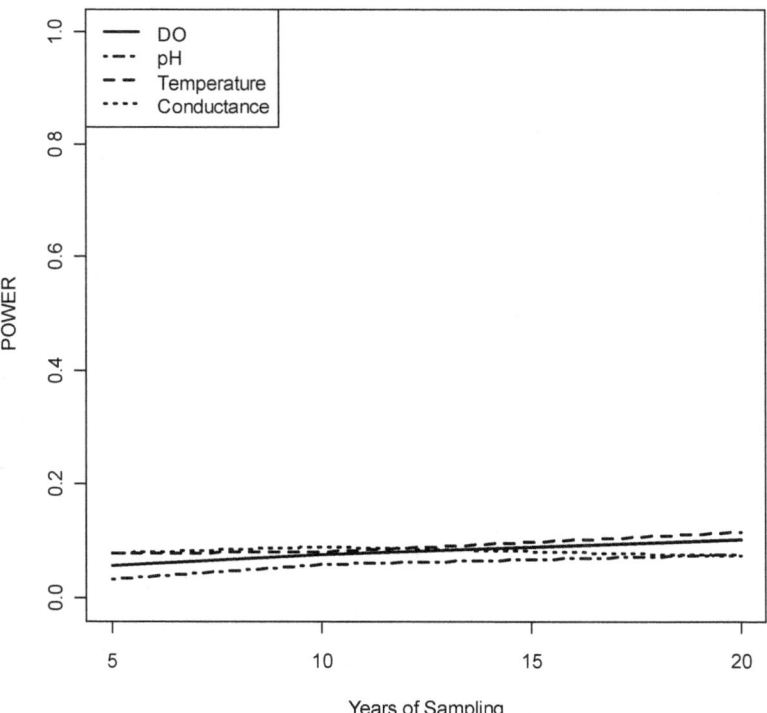

Figure 1.5. Probability of detecting trend for data simulated without trend at α=0.05 using the pilot data available from Snake River at Yellowstone National Park location. The estimated power using our methodology should be equivalent to the specified α-level.

21

Step 6: Iterations
Steps 3-5 are repeated for the number of iterations specified by the user.

Step 7: Determining Power
To determine the power of seasonal Kendall's τ (S) to detect trends in the parameter, we simply divide the number of 1s that occurred by the total number of iterations run.

Example
The estimated power for detecting a 2.5% annual change in temperature, conductivity, pH, and DO are shown for the Snake River YELL station in Figure 1.6. Based on Figure 1.6, we would conclude that we achieve 80% power to detect a 2.5% change in median DO sampling >5 years, with >8 years of sampling for conductance, and with >14 years of sampling for temperature. This assumes that there is at least one observation per season. If multiple observations were taken within a season, a median could be used in the seasonal Kendall test (see Chapter 2).

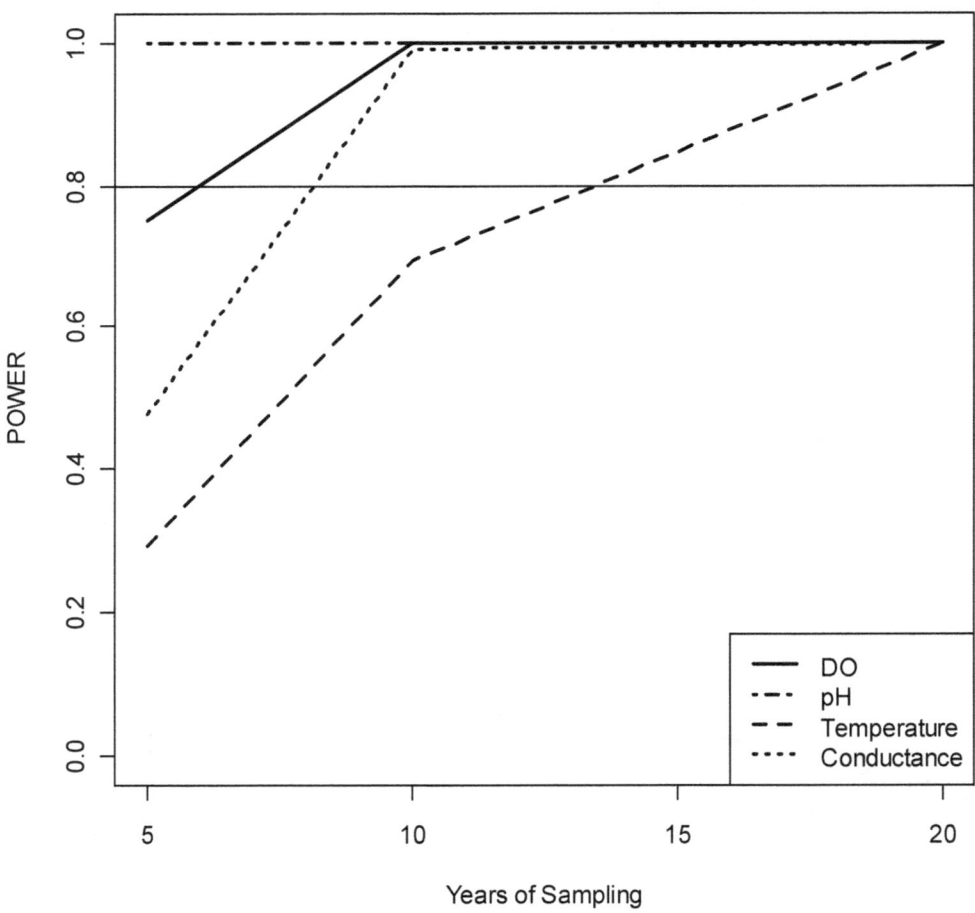

Figure 1.6. Estimated power of seasonal Kendall test to detect a 2.5% annual change in DO, pH, temperature, and conductance at the Snake River Yellowstone National Park location for 5, 10, and 20 years of sampling, using hydrograph seasons.

Discussion

In using our empirical bootstrap approach to estimate power for trend detection in water quality parameters of interest there are several things to keep in mind for its proper use. First, the validity and quantity of the input data that is used for re-sampling. The pilot data should be collected using the same instrumentation and QA/QC procedures as proposed in the future. Also there needs to be enough replicates within a season or within a month to "safely" use the bootstrapped distribution of the empirical residuals as an estimate of the true error distribution. The power function automatically generates a summary of the number of observations available within a season or within each month to assist with this assessment. As an extreme "what-if" example, say a researcher has 3 observations of DO in January gathered in 1998, 2001, 2005, so there are only 3 observations that are "recycled" in the code, it is possible the estimated power is too high because we are severely under-estimating the true variation in the data. As another example, if a researcher has 3 observations of DO gathered during 3 different weeks of January within the year 2000 these values are used in the same way in the power code, so the researcher needs to consider if this within season variation is representative of yearly variation for that season. Power is a function of the variability (noise) in the data, the power is higher for indicators with less variability. The user needs to carefully consider if the available data are representative of the expected variation and skewness into the future. Other options for conducting a power analysis are available that are based on assuming a statistical distribution for the data. The statistical distribution assumed for the data (a parametric bootstrap approach) can be informed and calibrated by pilot data.

Secondly, the user needs to thoughtfully consider what is a biologically meaningful annual rate of change in the water quality parameters of interest. Consider pH, we estimated that there was 100% power to detect a 2.5% annual change. This represents an unrealistically large degree of change over long time periods. For example, if pH starts at 7, within 20 years it will have increased to a median of 11.54; after 28 years at an annual rate of change of 2.5% the value exceeds 14 [$7*\exp(0.025*28)$]. This pattern is an artifact of how we are simulating data under the alternative hypothesis (with trend), it is possible for some water quality parameters the deterministic component we specified in Equation 1 is not appropriate. For practitioners' we suggest exploring the simulated data to determine if your annual rate of change and timeframe of interest make practical sense in the context of your long-term monitoring objectives. The code could be altered in the future to simulate data under a different model for the trend component if this step is a concern.

Another consideration is that we assume there are no non-detections or missing values in the pilot data. The power analysis code is not written to handle non-detects or missing values at present. The seasonal Kendall test can still be used when data are below the detection limit if the value is set to that lower limit for analysis and the detection limit has not changed over the years (Helsel and Hirsch 2002, Hirsh et al. 1982). If multiple observations fall below the detection limit, these ties can be accommodated by correcting the variance estimate (Helsel and Hirsch 2002, Hirsh et al. 1982). Flow weighting or flow adjustment should improve the ability to detect trend, so our estimates should be conservative for parameters that are highly positively correlated with flow (Alley 1988).

Chapter 2. Trend Analysis

The following implemented trend analysis procedures are based on Alley (1988) and Hirsch et al. (1982). In the accompanying R-code files in Appendix D, we have created two options, a seasonal Kendall test with and without flow adjustment. To demonstrate the use of this tool, we used a dataset for the lower Soda Butte site in YELL. The code was developed based on using the .csv file "Soda_Butte_lower_data.csv" as the input data file. A quick reference tutorial on the use of the code in Appendix D for a trend analysis is provided in Appendix E.

Data Format

The data were manipulated in Microsoft Excel to create a Julian date column, and a separate column for month, day, and year. For example, Table 2.1 displays the first three rows of data; the data should be formatted in the same way to use the R functions. The use of the Julian date avoids the issues with calendar dates in R and is a necessary input to sub-set the data into the pre-set seasons or months. In the R code, we create a day of the year which is then translated into months or hydrologic seasons. The user should verify that observations are being properly subset into the correct months or seasons, facilitated by the graphics that are automatically generated by the R code.

Table 2.1. First three rows of the csv file that can be used in the created R functions. The column names must be the same, otherwise the functions will not work correctly or at all. This is based on an NPS generated database known as NPStoret. Detailed instructions on the proper format for the data are provided in Appendix E.

Station ID	Visit Start Date	STORET Characteristic Name	Detection Condition	Result Value	Units	Detection Limit	Discharge (cfs)	Julian Date	Month	Day	Year
YELL_SB001.5M	6/15/2006	Sulfate	Detected and Quantified	3.16	mg/l	1	720	6166	6	15	2006
YELL_SB001.5M	7/12/2006	Magnesium	Detected and Quantified	6.76	mg/l	0.1	209	6193	7	12	2006

This particular dataset did not contain non-detect values. Our implementation of the seasonal Kendall test does not correct for ties in the data. If there are many ties due to multiple observations below the detection limit, the variance formula should be changed to that in Equation [12.10] in Helsel and Hirsch (2002). Also, if the detection limits have changed over the years resulting in multiple detection limits more sophisticated statistical methods should be used (see Helsel 2005 and the NADA package in R). The NADA package in R has an option for the Kendall test with censored data (function cenken).

Definition of Season for Trend Analysis
The hydrologic definition of seasons used in the R-code for the three parks are in Table 2.2 (same as Table 1.1). The user specifies which park the stream data correspond to (YELL, BICA or GRTE) and the season is defined accordingly.

Table 2.2. Hydrologic definition of seasons for the three parks within the GRYN.

	BICA	YELL	GRTE
1	August 10-April 14	November 1-April 15	August 15-April 14
2	April 15-June 19	April 16-June 15	April 15-June 9
3	June 20-August 9	June 16-August 15	June 10-August 14
4		August 16-October 31	

We assume that at least one observation is available per season for every year of sampling. If multiple observations are available, a median value is calculated within each season for analysis. The R code automatically calculates the median value based on multiple observations per season within a year. A warning message is issued if less than 10 years are available for analysis because the p-value is based on the asymptotic distribution of the test statistic which may not hold for less than 10 years of data. If this warning is issued, the user should consider using a bootstrap approach for hypothesis testing.

Option 1: Seasonal Kendall (no flow adjustment)

This is a nonparametric test that can be used to assess whether all seasons show the same trend over time. The details of this test were provided in Chapter 1. If trend within one particular season is of interest, a Kendall test should be used. The data would be the seasonal medians over time for that specific season. Using the seasonal Kendall test, it is possible to conclude there is no trend over time when, in fact, spring is increasing and winter is decreasing. The seasonal Kendall test is a test for concordant trends across seasons (parallel trend lines in the seasonal medians over years), but it is imperative to plot the data to properly interpret the p-values from a seasonal Kendall test and to understand the patterns in your data. Also, this test is appropriate if there is no relationship between discharge and the characteristic of interest over time. The latest version of the Kendall package in R includes a function for the seasonal Kendall test (function SeasonalMannKendall, release on Feb. 14, 2012).

Several plots are output from the R script we have created to facilitate data analysis for practitionars. Figure 2.1 displays the time series of the result values by Julian day, this graphic can be used to assess extreme observations that may be erroneous. Again the trend test implemented is non-parametric so outliers are not an issue, but the data should still be checked for data entry errors.

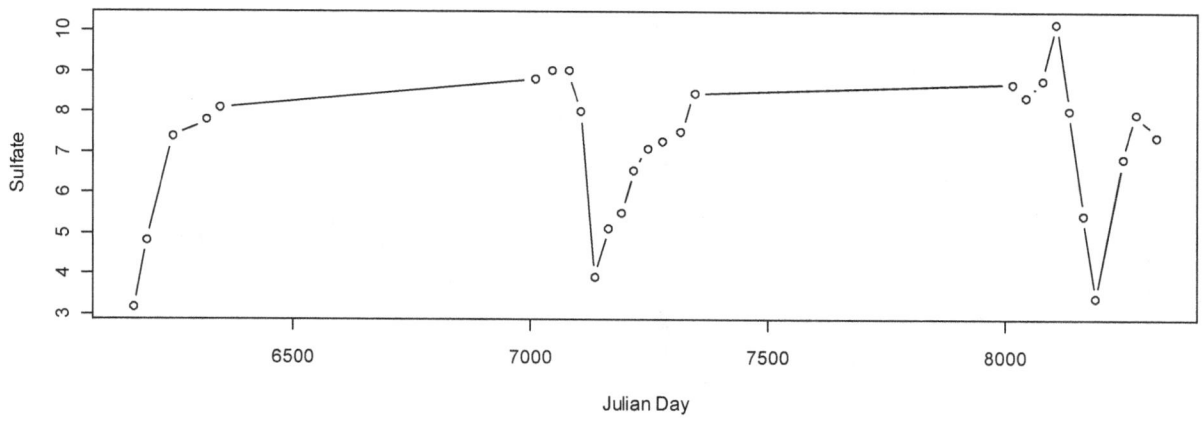

Figure 2.1. The sulfate characteristic values at Lower Soda Butte location in YELL versus Julian Day. This is a time series plot of the actual result values which is useful to assess possible data entry errors or other anomalies in data collection.

Figure 2.2 shows a scatterplot of sulfate versus discharge over time, this plot can be used to determine if flow adjustment is needed. In this example, there is a strong negative correlation suggesting that the flow adjustment procedure should be used (Corr=-0.86). The linear correlation coefficient is automatically calculated, but should only be interpreted if the graphic (Figure 2.2.) displays a linear relationship.

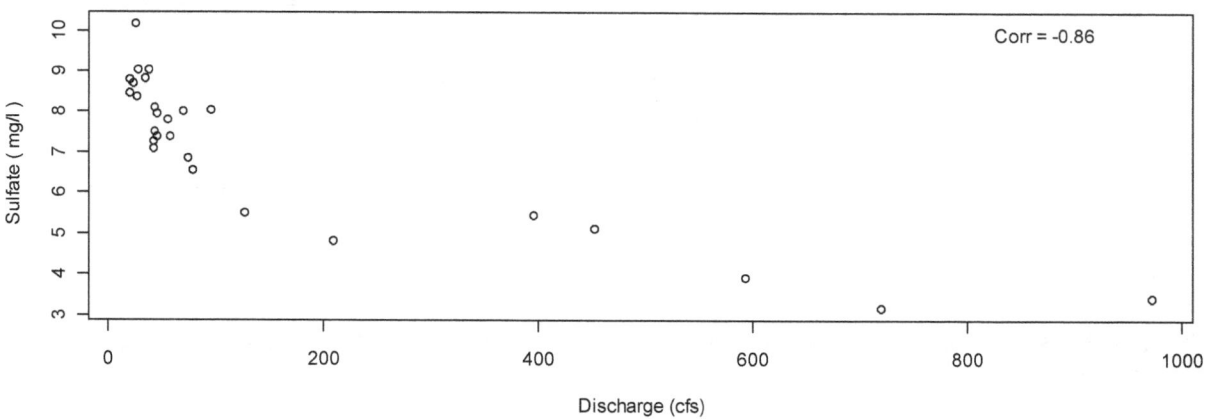

Figure 2.2. Sulfate (mg/L) characteristic values versus discharge (cfs) collected at Lower Soda Butte location in YELL. Notice for sulfate there is evidence of a negative correlation between sulfate (mg/L) and discharge (cfs), suggesting the appropriate analysis is to adjust for flow.

Figures 2.3 and 2.4 provide additional displays of the data that may be of interest if monthly versus hydrograph seasons are used to sub-set the data. These boxplots are pooling over years, so even if there were a trend it would not be evident in these plots. However, these plots provide an assessment of the patterns in the medians over seasons or months and whether the variability is constant and if there are any outliers present.

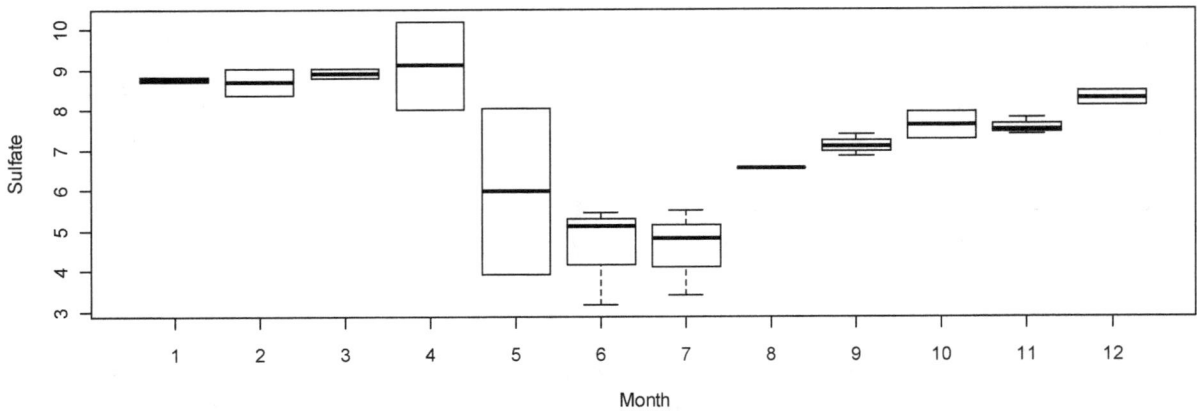

Figure 2.3. Monthly boxplots of characteristic of interest, here Sulfate (mg/L) at Lower Soda Butte location in YELL. This plot shows variability changes across the months as does the median values.

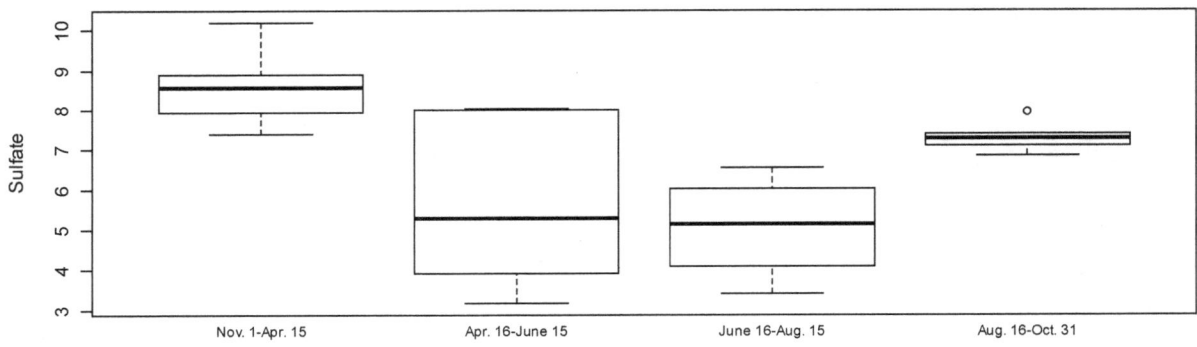

Figure 2.4. Seasonal boxplot of characteristic of interest, here Sulfate (mg/L) at Lower Soda Butte location in YELL.

Figure 2.5 should be used to properly interpret the p-value, if the p-value is large (>0.10) suggesting there is no evidence of trend, it could be because the seasons have opposite patterns (increasing and decreasing over years) as opposed to the same pattern for all seasons across years. The seasonal Kendall test is testing for evidence of concordant trend over the seasons (parallel trend lines in the medians). In this example, there appears to be a negative trend in median sulfate in season 3 (June 16-August 15), an increasing trend in median Sulfate in season 2 (April 16-June 15), and no trend in seasons 1 (November 1-April 15) and 4 (August 16-October 31) median values.

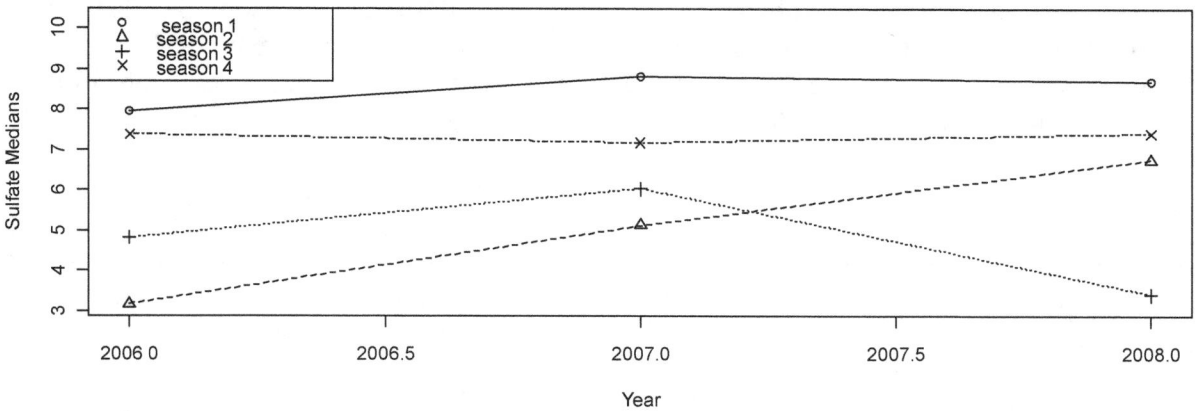

Figure 2.5. Seasonal medians of sulfate over years by season. These median values are the data used in the seasonal Kendall test without flow adjustment.

Option 2: Seasonal Kendall on the Residuals (flow adjustment)

We also provide the option of flow adjustment for those parameters (such as Sulfate in Figure 2.2) that covary with discharge. We make the flow adjustment by first calculating the residuals (res_{ijl}) for the lth observation in the jth season and i^{th} year from a simple linear regression model with the predictor variable discharge (X=Discharge) as follows,

$$res_{ijl} = (Y_{ijl} - \hat{\beta}_{0j} + \hat{\beta}_{1j}X_{ijl}), \qquad (2)$$

where Y_{ijl} indexes the lth observation in the jth season and i^{th} year, and we assume the characteristic of interest has a unique linear relationship with discharge ($\hat{\beta}_{0j} + \hat{\beta}_{1j}$) for each season j. The medians of the residuals per season and year combination are then calculated in the case of $l > 1$, and these medians are the "data" inputs to the seasonal Kendall test.

The seasonal Kendall test on the residuals has two main assumptions that should be verified:

(A1) there is no trend in discharge over time, and

(A2) there is a significant linear relationship between discharge and the characteristic of interest.

The assumptions hold based on the sulfate pilot data provided. However, the sample size (number of years) is very small for some seasons in the data from Soda Butte (for example, only two years had values for Magnesium sampled between April 16 to June 15), which suggests low power to ascertain if this is an appropriate assumption. The R script function automatically creates plots that can be used to assess the assumptions stated above.

There are several warning messages included in the R function because of our concern over the potential misuse of a p-value without considering whether the assumptions are met for the test to be valid. Alley (1988) lays out the framework for when this approach should be used. If there is a

29

significant relationship between year and discharge, a different approach should be used. Also, the R code is currently written to adjust for discharge within each season. Note the results change if we assume the same relationship between discharge and sulfate across seasons. The R function with flow adjustment selected produces the same Figure 2.2 and additional exploratory plots of discharge. Specifically, discharge by season and year to assess whether there is evidence of a yearly trend in discharge (Figure 2.6).

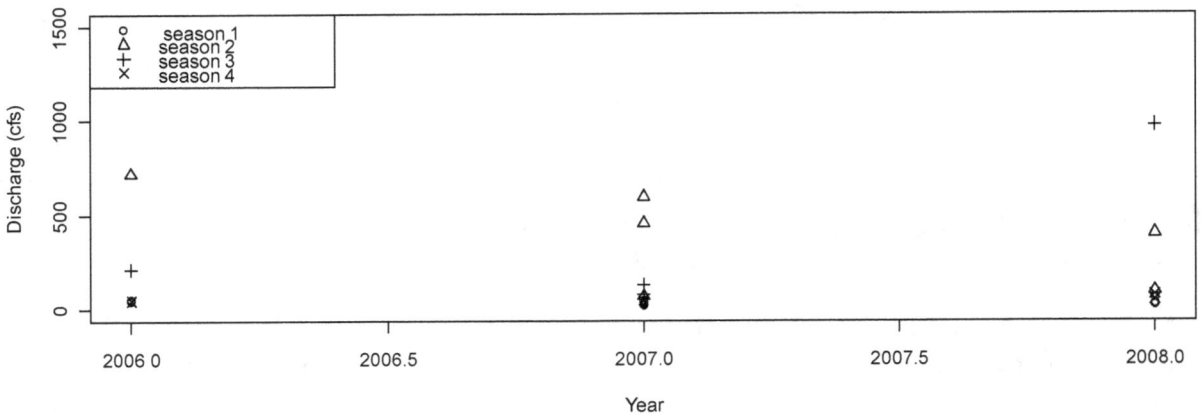

Figure 2.6. Discharge (cfs) recorded at the Lower Soda Butte location in YELL coded by season across years.

Based on Figure 2.6, we would conclude there there doesn't appear to be a trend in discharge over years.

There is evidence that the relationship between discharge and sulfate varies by season (Figure 2.7). The R code as written is adjusting for flow appropriately. Again the R code can be modified if this model for discharge needs to be altered and we refer the reader to Helsel and Hirsch (2002) and Libiseller and Grimvall (2002) for other approaches.

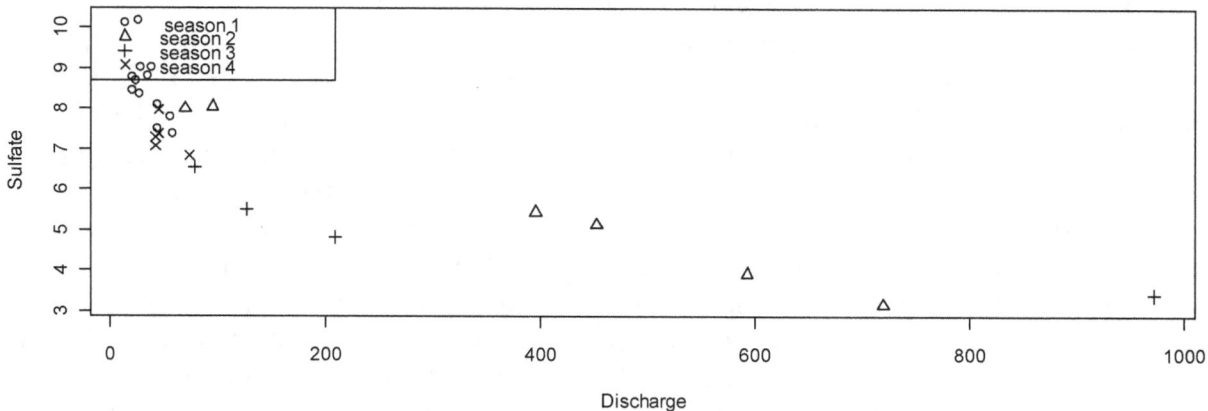

Figure 2.7. Sulfate versus discharge recorded at the Lower Soda Butte location in YELL coded by season.

Figure 2.8 displays the data used in the seasonal Kendall test on the residuals after flow adjustment.

Again, a key assumption is that there is no trend in discharge across years and we are assuming that the data gathered within each season has a different linear relationship with discharge in the adjustment. These assumptions could be modified in the R code in Appendix D if necessary. Appendix E provides a step-by-step example for a trend analysis of Sulfate at Soda Butte.

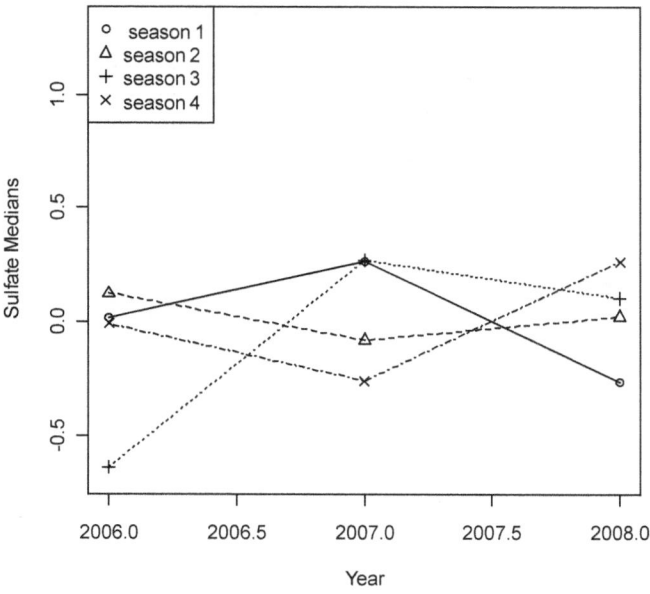

Figure 2.8. Median sulfate after adjusting for discharge across years with different symbols for season for the Lower Soda Butte location in YELL.

Discussion

We have developed R code to automate some routine methods used to detect trends in water quality parameters based on Alley (1988) and Hirsch et al. (1982). However, there are several assumptions that need to be verified when interpreting the output. We provide some routine graphics to assist with assessing these assumptions. To reiterate, the seasonal Kendall test assumes that at least one observation is available within each season and year, if this is not true the code will fail to run. Also, the test is for evidence of concordant seasonal trends over time. Importantly, for those parameters that may vary as a function of discharge we provide a flow adjustment option in the R code. The hypothesis test is implemented based on a large sample assumption; however, if less than 10 years of data are available a bootstrap approach could be used for hypothesis testing. Also, if censored observations are an issue the user should consult the NADA package in R that accompanies Helsel (2005), the NADA package includes a function for the Kendall test for censored observations. Our implementation is sufficient for only one detection limit, but for water quality parameters with multiple detection limits other statistical techniques should be explored.

Conclusions

This report outlines two statistical tools developed specifically for the GRYN water resources vital sign. However, we feel these tools will benefit other networks that are interested in site-specific trends in water quality parameters. Our power analysis procedures can be used to determine whether monthly or seasonal sampling yields the same power for trend detection, a key trade-off that might lead to overall reduction in costs for a program. We have implemented the commonly used methods for trend detection in water quality monitoring, but a mixed effects model could be used when multiple sites are surveyed over years, if regional trends are of interest, and error distributions appear normally distributed (Starcevich et al. [in review]). If non-normality of the residuals is an issue, a regional Kendall test could be explored in the case of multiple sites sampled over time (Helsel and Frans 2006).

Literature Cited

Alley, W. M. 1988. Using exogenous variables in testing for monotonic trends in hydrologic time series. *Water Resources Research* 24(11):1955-1961.

Buhl-Mortensen, L. 1996. Type-II statistical errors in environmental science and the precautionary principle. *Marine Pollution Bulletin* 32(7): 528-531.

Fancy, S. G., J. E. Gross, and S. L. Carter. 2008. Monitoring the condition of natural resources in U.S. national parks. *Environmental Monitoring and Assessment* 151:161–174.

Gibbs, J. P., S. Droege, and P. Eagle, 1998. Monitoring populations of plants and animals. *BioScience* 48(11):935-940.

Helsel, D. R. 2005. *Nondetects and Data Analysis.* New Jersey: John Wiley and Sons, Inc.

Helsel, D. R. and L. M. Frans. 2006. Regional Kendall test for trend. *Environmental Science and Technology* 40: 4066-4073.

Helsel, D. R. and R. M. Hirsch. 2002. *Statistical Methods in Water Resources.* U.S. Geological Survey. City, State. http://water.usgs.gov/pubs/twri/twri4a3/

Hirsch, R. M., J. R. Slack, and R. A. Smith. 1982. Techniques of trend analysis for monthly water quality data. *Water Resources Research* 18(1):107-121.

Jean, C., A. M. Schrag, R. E. Bennetts, R. Daley, E. A. Crowe, and S. O'Ney. 2005. Vital Signs Monitoring Plan for the Greater Yellowstone Network. National Park Service, Fort Collins, Colorado.

Kendall, M. G. 1975. *Rank Correlation Methods.* Charles Griffin, London.

Libiseller, C. and A. Grimvall. 2002. Performance of partial Mann-Kendall tests for trend detection in the presence of covariates. *Environmetrics* 13:71-84.

Mapstone, B. D. 1995. Scalable decision rules for environmetal impact studies: effect size, Type I, and Type II errors. *Ecological Applications* 5(2):401-410.

O'Ney S. E., J. Arnold, C. Bromley, R. Daley, C. Jean, and S. Ostermann-Kelm. 2009 [in review]. Greater Yellowstone Network water resource monitoring protocol: Version 1.0. Natural Resource Report NPS/GRN/NRR—2009/XXX. National Park Service, Fort Collins, Colorado.

O'Ney S. E. 2006. Regulatory water quality monitoring protocol. Version 2.0. Bozeman (MT): National Park Service Greater Yellowstone Network.

Starcevich, L. A., Irvine, K. M. and A. M. Heard (in review) Impacts of temporal revisit designs on the power to detect trend with a linear mixed model: an application to long-term monitoring of Sierra Nevada Lakes. *Environmental Monitoring and Assessment.*

Yue, S. and P. Pilon. 2004 A comparison of the power of the *t*-test, Mann-Kendall and bootstrap tests for trend detection. *Hydrological sciences-Journal-des Sciences Hydrologiques* 49(1):21-37.

Appendix A: Power Analysis Data Preparation

An example input dataset (first 5 rows) for the power code is shown in Table A1.

Table A1. Example input data needed for the power analysis.

Location	Date	ParamGroup	Result	JulianDate
Snake_River	5/29/2002	Conductance	85	2149
Snake_River	5/29/2002	DO	9.5	2149
Snake_River	5/29/2002	pH	7.7	2149
Snake_River	5/29/2002	Temperature	5.2	2149

The data used in the example for Snake River at YELL location were only those observations since 2002.

The following data preparation steps were done in Microsoft Excel prior to loading the data in R.

1) The data should be subset to the particular location of interest.

2) All non-detects should be removed. Only rows with an actual number for the result column can be used in the power code.

3) The ParamGroup variable should be consistent across observations, for example "water temp-field" and "water temp" need to be changed to a common name such as Temperature.

4) A JulianDate field (column) needs to be added. This was accomplished using the following formula in Excel=**RIGHT(YEAR(A1),2)&TEXT(A1-DATE(YEAR(A1),1,0),"000")**. This converts a date in cell A1 to a Julian Date. This formula is from the website http://www.cpearson.com/excel/jdates.htm. The website description is "This formula takes the 2 right-most characters of the YEAR of the date in A1, and then appends the number of days between the date in A1 and the 0th day of that year. The TEXT function formats the day-of-year number as three digits, with leading zeros if necessary."

5) For the R-code to run, the column headings need to be the same for "ParamGroup", "Result", and "JulianDate." Verify this is true.

6) The Excel file should be saved as a comma delimited file with extension .csv.

Appendix B: R-Code for Power Analysis

```
# Power Code for GRYN Water Quality Power Analysis
# Author: Kathi Irvine and Cynthia Hollimon
# Date: March 2012


        # The following power code can be used to determine the power of the Seasonal Mann-Kendall
test for detecting a given
        # magnitude of trend.
        # The procedure requires historic data to re-sample from in order to estimate power.
        # Also, the definition of season needs to be input by the user, typically based on the hydrograph.
        # We assume that one observation per season is available.


        # SUBMIT THE FOLLOWING LINES OF CODE FROM
        # HERE TO

library(Kendall)

        ## Kendall Functions
        power.kendall<-function (x, y) {
          tau <- 0
          ptau <- 0
          sltau <- 0
    score <- 0
    varscore <- 0
    denom <- 0
    i <- ! (is.na(x) | is.na(y))
    x <- x[i]
    y <- y[i]
    iws <- numeric (length(x) )
    ifault <- 0
    outF <- .Fortran("tauk2", as.single(x), as.single(y), as.integer(length(x)),
        as.single(tau), as.single(ptau), as.single(sltau), as.single(score),
        as.single(varscore), as.single(denom), as.integer(iws),
        as.integer(ifault), PACKAGE = "Kendall")
    tau <- outF[[4]]
    sl <- outF[[6]]
    sc <- outF[[7]]
    var.sc <- outF[[8]]
    denom <- outF[[9]]
    ier <- outF[[11]]
    ans <- list(tau = tau, sl = sl, S = sc, D = denom, varS = var.sc)
    oldClass(ans) <- "Kendall"
    ans
```

```
}

power.MannKendall<-function (x) {
   power.kendall(1:length(x), x)
}


Power.fun<-
function(data.in,alpha.level,nboot,change.of.interest,no.years,param.assigned,season.location,seasons,month.compare){


   # INPUTS FOR POWER FUNCTION
   #      data.in=
   #      alpha.level
   #      nboot
   #      change.of.interest
   #      no.years
   #      param.assigned
   #      season.location
   #      seasons
   #      month.compare


   # definitions of hydrologic seasons

   #BICA: Aug 10-April 14, April 15 - June 19, June 20- Aug. 9
   #YELL: Nov 1 - April 15, April 16-June 15, June 16- Aug 15, Aug 16- Oct 31
   #GRTE: Aug 15-April 14, April 15-June 9, June 10-Aug. 14

   # translating to day of the year

    seasons.GRTE<-c(228,105,106,161,162,227)
    seasons.YELL<-c(306, 106,107,167,168,228,229,305)
    seasons.BICA<-c(223,105,106,171,172,222)

   # defining months instead of seasons

    months <-
c(1,31,32,60,61,91,92,121,122,152,153,182,183,213,214,244,245,274,275,305,306,335,336,366)


   ###     subsettting to the parameter of interest

              param1<-subset(data.in,data.in$ParamGroup==param.assigned)

              # creating a season variable
```

```r
day.of.year<-as.numeric(substr(param1$JulianDate,2,6))

# may need to be altered for different season definitions

if(missing(season.location)) season.intervals <- months else
        if(season.location=="GRTE") season.intervals<-seasons.GRTE  else
                if(season.location=="YELL") season.intervals<-seasons.YELL  else
                        season.intervals<-seasons.BICA

if(length(season.intervals)/(2*seasons)!=1) print("Error Number of Seasons and Season Location
do not match")

if(month.compare == T | missing(season.location)) {month.var <- numeric()  #setting up month
vars for comparison
        for(i in 1:length(day.of.year)) {
        {
        if(day.of.year[i] >=months[1]&day.of.year[i]<=months[2]) month.var[i] <- 1 else
        if(day.of.year[i] >=months[3]&day.of.year[i]<=months[4]) month.var[i] <- 2 else
        if(day.of.year[i] >=months[5]&day.of.year[i]<=months[6]) month.var[i] <- 3 else
        if(day.of.year[i] >=months[7]&day.of.year[i]<=months[8]) month.var[i] <- 4 else
        if(day.of.year[i] >=months[9]&day.of.year[i]<=months[10]) month.var[i] <- 5 else
        if(day.of.year[i] >=months[11]&day.of.year[i]<=months[12]) month.var[i] <- 6 else
        if(day.of.year[i] >=months[13]&day.of.year[i]<=months[14]) month.var[i] <- 7 else
        if(day.of.year[i] >=months[15]&day.of.year[i]<=months[16]) month.var[i] <- 8 else
        if(day.of.year[i] >=months[17]&day.of.year[i]<=months[18]) month.var[i] <- 9 else
        if(day.of.year[i] >=months[19]&day.of.year[i]<=months[20]) month.var[i] <- 10 else
        if(day.of.year[i] >=months[21]&day.of.year[i]<=months[22]) month.var[i] <- 11 else
        if(day.of.year[i] >=months[23]&day.of.year[i]<=months[24]) month.var[i] <- 12}}}


if(missing(season.location)) {season.var <- month.var} else  #if running only a monthly analysis

if(season.location=="GRTE"|season.location=="BICA") {season.var<-numeric()
        for(i in 1:length(day.of.year))

{if(day.of.year[i]<=season.intervals[2]|day.of.year[i]>=season.intervals[1]) season.var[i]<-1 else

if(day.of.year[i]>=season.intervals[3]&day.of.year[i]<=season.intervals[4]) season.var[i]<-2 else

if(day.of.year[i]>=season.intervals[5]&day.of.year[i]<=season.intervals[6]) season.var[i]<-3}} else

        if(season.location=="YELL")  {season.var<-numeric()
                for(i in 1:length(day.of.year))
                {

if(day.of.year[i]<=season.intervals[2]|day.of.year[i]>=season.intervals[1]) season.var[i]<-1 else

if(day.of.year[i]>=season.intervals[3]&day.of.year[i]<=season.intervals[4]) season.var[i]<-2 else
```

```
if(day.of.year[i]>=season.intervals[5]&day.of.year[i]<=season.intervals[6]) season.var[i]<-3 else

if(day.of.year[i]>=season.intervals[7]&day.of.year[i]<=season.intervals[8]) season.var[i]<-4
                    }}
```

```
        Power.out<-
function(data.in,alpha.level,nboot,change.of.interest,no.years,param.assigned,season.location,seasons,s
eason.var){ #new function loop

                            ## Determine median values for the different seasons

                medians<-tapply(param1$Result,season.var,median)

            ## Find a set of epsilon stars based on medians. keep residuals within Seasons!
                epsilons<-rep(NA,dim(param1)[1])
                epsilons<- param1$Result-medians[as.character(season.var)]

                    # de-trended by seasonal medians


                    # Build a bunch of storage objects

                        tau<-
array(NA,dim=c(length(unique(season.var)),nboot,(length(no.years))))
                        sktau<-matrix(NA,nrow=nboot,ncol=(length(no.years)))
                        ts.out<-matrix(NA,nrow=nboot,ncol=(length(no.years)))
                        sim.out<-
matrix(NA,nrow=nboot,ncol=(length(no.years)))
                        S<-
array(NA,dim=c(length(unique(season.var)),nboot,(length(no.years))))
                        power<-rep(NA,(length(no.years)))
                        power.mat<-
matrix(NA,(length(change.of.interest)),(length(no.years)))


            # Calculate denominator of Z-statistic for each timecut (since it's based on
sample size alone, we can do it at this point)
            # this is a normal approximation to the distribution of the test-statistic as stated in
equation 8

                        denom.mat<-rep(NA,(length(no.years)))
                        for(j in 1:length(no.years)){
                            denom.mat[j]<-no.years[j]*(no.years[j]-1)*(2*no.years[j]+5)/18
                            }

                denom.vec<-denom.mat*length(unique(season.var))
```

```
# For each change.of.interest

for(h in 1:length(change.of.interest)){

# Begin bootstrapping
    for(i in 1:nboot){

# TIME LOOP
    for(j in 1:length(no.years)){

years<-0:(no.years[j]-1)  #years in this run

# Simulating realistic data with monotonic non-linear trend
# using T2 as defined in Eq 5b of Yue and Pilon 2004
# requires B2= baseline median each season, a2=multiplicative change for each one year
increase in time

fixed.trend<-exp(change.of.interest[h]*years)


#bootstrap the residuals within a season to add onto the fixed.trend vector

boot.eps<-
tapply(epsilons,season.var,sample,length(years),replace=TRUE)

# create one realization of a time series for each season

for(k in 1:length(unique(season.var))){
    boot.by.seas<-
medians[k]*fixed.trend+boot.eps[[k]]


# Calculate tau and S within each season and each timecut using the
MannKendall function from package Kendall (see comment below)
    out<-power.MannKendall(boot.by.seas)

tau[k,i,j]<-out$tau
S[k,i,j]<-out$S
        }

# Calculate test statistic by #summing over
seasons and dividing by appropriate sqrt(denominator)
# See Hirsch et al. 1982 Water Resources Research Eqn. 8 and 9

sktau[i,j]<-sum(S[,i,j])
ts.out[i,j]<-
ifelse(sktau[i,j]>=0,(sktau[i,j]-
1)/sqrt(denom.vec[j]),(sktau[i,j]+1)/sqrt(denom.vec[j]))
```

43

```r
                                    # Collect a 1 if null (no trend) is rejected; a 0 otherwise for both methods.
                                        sim.out[i,j]<-
ifelse(abs(ts.out[i,j])>=qnorm(1-alpha.level),1,0)
                                                } #end of j loop
                            }               # end of i loop


                    ## Section 4: Calculate Power
                                    # Sum up number of times null was rejected within each timecut and
divide by the number of bootstraps to get power under each method.
                                        for(r in 1:(length(no.years))){
                                                power[r]<-sum(sim.out[,r])/nboot
                                        }
                                        power.mat[h,] <- power
                            } #end of h loop


                    if(month.compare == F| length(unique(season.var)) <= 4) {
                                plot(1,ylim=c(0,1),xlim=c(min(no.years)-1,max(no.years)+1),type="l",xlab="Years
of Data Collection",ylab="Power",main=paste("Power to Detect Various Annual % Changes in",
param.assigned,sep=" "))
                                    abline(h=.8,lty=2)
                                    for(i in 1:length(change.of.interest)){
                                            points(no.years,power.mat[i,],pch=i)
                                            lines(no.years,power.mat[i,],lty=1)
                                            if(month.compare==F & length(unique(season.var)) <= 4) {leg.text =
c(paste("Seasonal",change.of.interest*100,"%",sep=" "))
                                                            points=(1:length(change.of.interest))
                                                            lines=1} else
                                                    if(month.compare==F & length(unique(season.var)) > 4)
{leg.text = c(paste("Monthly",change.of.interest*100,"%",sep=" "))
                                                            points=(1:length(change.of.interest))
                                                            lines=1} else
                                                    leg.text =
c(paste("Seasonal",change.of.interest*100,"%",sep=" "),paste("Monthly",change.of.interest*100,"%",sep="
"))
                                                            points=rep(1:length(change.of.interest),2)
                                                            lines=rep(1:2,
each=length(change.of.interest))
                                            }
                                            legend("bottomright",legend=leg.text,pch=c(points),lty=c(lines))
                                    }                               else

                            for(i in 1:length(change.of.interest)){
                                    points(no.years,power.mat[i,],pch=i)
                                    lines(no.years,power.mat[i,],lty=2)
                                    }


            # output the number of observations available for the bootstrap within season
            no.obs<-table(season.var)
```

44

```
                    list.out<-list(param.assigned, seasons, no.years, alpha.level, nboot,
change.of.interest, power.mat,no.obs)
                    names(list.out)<-c("Parameter","Number of Seasons","Years of Data
Collection","Alpha","Iterations","Annual Rate of Change ","Power","No. Obs. Available")
                    return(list.out)


    }


    season.out <-
Power.out(data.in,alpha.level,nboot,change.of.interest,no.years,param.assigned,season.location,seasons
,season.var)

        if(month.compare == T) {month.out <-
Power.out(data.in,alpha.level,nboot,change.of.interest,no.years,param.assigned,season.location,seasons
=12,season.var=month.var)

    }

        if(month.compare == T) {list.out.all <- c(season.out,month.out)} else
            list.out.all <- season.out
            return(list.out.all)

    }



    ## END POWER FUNCTIONS

    ## HERE
```

Appendix C: Example Step-by-Step Use of R-Code for Power Analysis

Step 1. Follow directions in Appendix A for data preparation steps.

Step 2. Open the R program; change the working directory to the location containing the data files and R-code for the power analysis (Appendix B code). R code can be saved as a .txt file or .R file. We have provided the file "GRYN_power_code_KI_Oct2010.R" which is a duplicate of the code in Appendix B.

Step 3. Install R package Kendall, instructions can be found in Appendix F.

Step 4. Open the file containing the power analysis code ("GRYN_power_code_ Mar2012.R")

Step 5. Highlight all of the text in the file ("GRYN_power_code_KI_Oct2010.R"). Then on the top toolbar under the "Edit" option select "run all." This step creates the following functions in R: Power.fun, power.kendall, power.MannKendall.

Step 6. Open file "GRYN_Example_PowerCommands_Mar2012.R."

Step 7. Input the data from step 1 using the following commands:

```
data.in<-read.csv("SnakeOnly_data_2002_2009_years.csv",header=T)
attach(data.in)
names(data.in)
```

Step 8. The following inputs are required to run the power code:

data.in = pilot data set to use from step 1
alpha.level= type 1 error rate (usually 0.10)
nboot= number of iterations (usually 1000)
change.of.interest = annual multiplicative change in medians (0.025 for 2.5% increase)
no.years= number of years of sampling (e.g., 5, 10, 20)
param.assigned = parameter of interest (e.g., temperature)
season.location = GRTE or YELL or BICA or removed to run a monthly analysis
seasons = number of seasons 3 or 4 or 12 to run a monthly analysis
month.compare = T to compare seasonal analysis to a finer, monthly scale or F to run power analysis without a comparison

Example code for estimating the power to detect a 1% and 2.5% annual change in Temperature for 5, 10, and 20 years of sampling with seasonal sampling as compared to monthly sampling:

Power.fun(data.in,alpha.level=.1,nboot=1000,change.of.interest=c(.01,.025),no.years=c(5,10,20),param.a
ssigned=as.character("Temperature"),season.location=as.character("YELL"),seasons=4,month.compare=
T)

Example of output from "Power.fun" function:

$Parameter
[1] "Temperature"

$`Number of Seasons`
[1] 4

$`Years of Data Collection`
[1] 5 10 20

$Alpha
[1] 0.1

$Iterations
[1] 1000

$`Annual Rate of Change `
[1] 0.010 0.025

$Power
     [,1] [,2] [,3]
[1,] 0.207 0.388 0.842
[2,] 0.306 0.691 1.000

$`No. Obs. Available`
season.var
 1 2 3 4
17 21 28 30

$Parameter
[1] "Temperature"

$`Number of Seasons`
[1] 12

$`Years of Data Collection`
[1] 5 10 20

$Alpha
[1] 0.1

$Iterations
[1] 1000

$`Annual Rate of Cha ige `
[1] 0.010 0.025

$Power
      [,1] [,2] [,3]
[1,] 0.704 0.987   1
[2,] 0.824 1.000   1

$`No. Obs. Available`
season.var
 1 2 4 5 6 7 8 9 10 11 12
 3 2 3 8 15 15 13 15 10 9 3

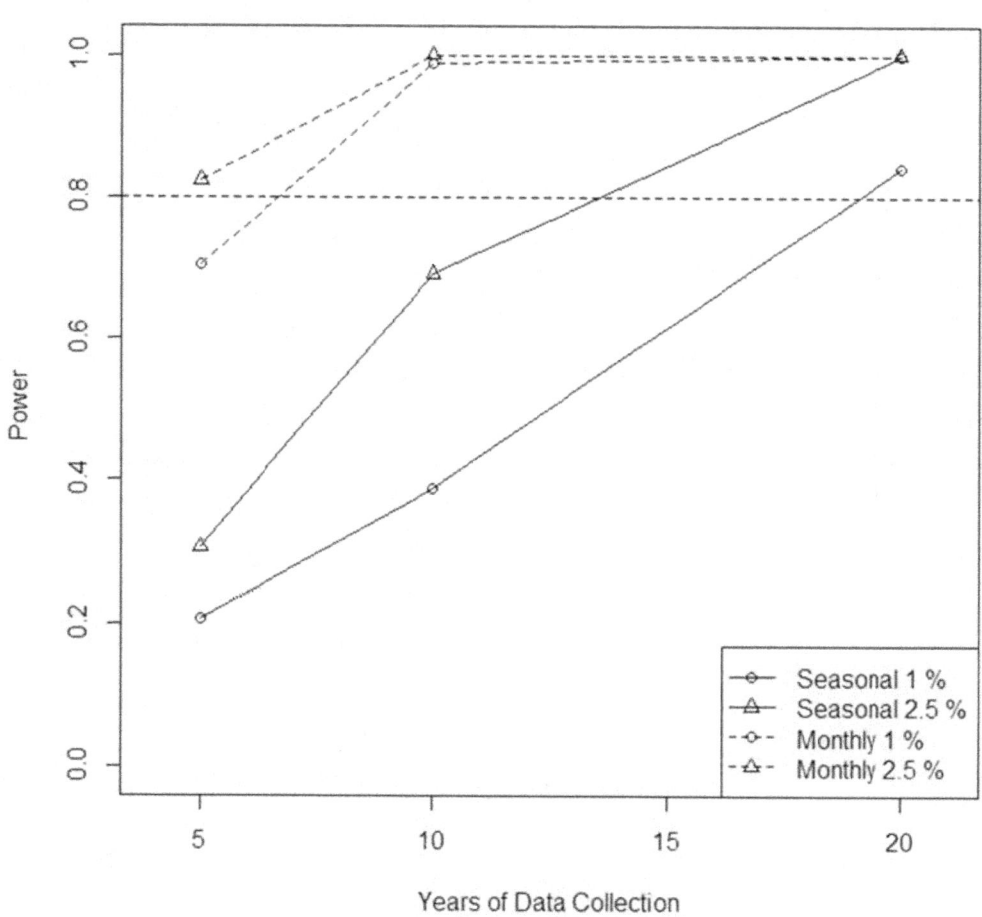

Figure C1. Example plot comparing the power to detect different magnitu les of trend under monthly and seasonal sampling of temperature.

Appendix D: R-Code for Trend Analysis Functions

```
# Written by K. Irvine and Cynthia Hollimon
# March 2012
# Functions for
# 1. seasonal Mann-Kendall test and
# 2. seasonal Mann-Kendall test adjusted for flow (Alley 1988)
# See accompanying document GRYN_WaterTrendAnalysisExample_2011Feb1_KI.doc

## WRAPPER FUNCTION

library(Kendall)

GRYN.TREND.WATER<-function(data.input,VarName,season.location,no.season,TEST){

        #subsetting the data
        SubData<-subset(data.input, STORET.Characteristic.Name==VarName)


        # Time series plots
windows()
        plot(SubData$JulianDate,SubData$Result.Value,type='b',xlab="Julian
Day",ylab=paste(VarName),pch=21,bg=1,lwd=2)

        #OVERALL VS BY SEASON
windows()
        plot(SubData$Discharge..cfs.,SubData$Result.Value,xlab="Discharge
(cfs)",ylab=paste(VarName,"(",SubData$Units[1],")"),pch=21,bg=1)
        text(max(SubData$Discharge..cfs.)-100,10,paste("Corr
=" ,round(cor(SubData$Discharge..cfs.,SubData$Result.Value),2)))

#monthly boxplot
windows()
boxplot(SubData$Result.Value~SubData$Month,xlab="Month",varwidth=T,ylab=paste(VarNam
e))



        #CREATING SEASONAL VARIABLE

    day.of.year<-as.numeric(substr(SubData$JulianDate,2,6))


#BICA: Aug 10-April 14, April 15 - June 19, June 20- Aug. 9
#YELL: Nov 1 - April 15, April 16-June 15, June 16- Aug 15, Aug 16- Oct 31
#GRTE: Aug 15-April 14, April 15-June 9, June 10-Aug. 14

# translating to day of the year
```

```r
seasons.GRTE<-c(228,105,106,161,162,227)
seasons.YELL<-c(306, 106,107,167,168,228,229,305)
seasons.BICA<-c(223,105,106,171,172,222)

# defining months instead of seasons

 months <-
c(1,31,32,60,61,91,92,121,122,152,153,182,183,213,214,244,245,274,275,305,306,335,336,36
6)


# may need to be altered for different season definitions



if(missing(season.location)) season.intervals <- months else
    if(season.location=="GRTE") season.intervals<-seasons.GRTE  else
    if(season.location=="YELL") season.intervals<-seasons.YELL  else
       season.intervals<-seasons.BICA



### assigning numbers for month variables

if(missing(season.location)) {season.var <- numeric()
    for(i in 1:length(day.of.year))
       {
       if(day.of.year[i] >=season.intervals[1]&day.of.year[i]<=season.intervals[2]) season.var[i]
<- 1 else
       if(day.of.year[i] >=season.intervals[3]&day.of.year[i]<=season.intervals[4]) season.var[i]
<- 2 else
       if(day.of.year[i] >=season.intervals[5]&day.of.year[i]<=season.intervals[6]) season.var[i]
<- 3 else
       if(day.of.year[i] >=season.intervals[7]&day.of.year[i]<=season.intervals[8]) season.var[i]
<- 4 else
       if(day.of.year[i] >=season.intervals[9]&day.of.year[i]<=season.intervals[10]) season.var[i]
<- 5 else
       if(day.of.year[i] >=season.intervals[11]&day.of.year[i]<=season.intervals[12])
season.var[i] <- 6 else
       if(day.of.year[i] >=season.intervals[13]&day.of.year[i]<=season.intervals[14])
season.var[i] <- 7 else
       if(day.of.year[i] >=season.intervals[15]&day.of.year[i]<=season.intervals[16])
season.var[i] <- 8 else
       if(day.of.year[i] >=season.intervals[17]&day.of.year[i]<=season.intervals[18])
season.var[i] <- 9 else
       if(day.of.year[i] >=season.intervals[19]&day.of.year[i]<=season.intervals[20])
season.var[i] <- 10 else
       if(day.of.year[i] >=season.intervals[21]&day.of.year[i]<=season.intervals[22])
season.var[i] <- 11 else
       if(day.of.year[i] >=season.intervals[23]&day.of.year[i]<=season.intervals[24])
season.var[i] <- 12}} else
```

```
if(season.location=="GRTE"|season.location=="BICA") {season.var<-numeric()
    for(i in 1:length(day.of.year))
        {
            if(day.of.year[i]<=season.intervals[2]|day.of.year[i]>=season.intervals[1])
season.var[i]<-1 else
        if(day.of.year[i]>=season.intervals[3]&day.of.year[i]<=season.intervals[4]) season.var[i]<-
2 else
        if(day.of.year[i]>=season.intervals[5]&day.of.year[i]<=season.intervals[6]) season.var[i]<-
3}} else

if(season.location=="YELL") {season.var<-numeric()
    for(i in 1:length(day.of.year))
        {
        if(day.of.year[i]<=season.intervals[2]|day.of.year[i]>=season.intervals[1]) season.var[i]<-1
else
        if(day.of.year[i]>=season.intervals[3]&day.of.year[i]<=season.intervals[4]) season.var[i]<-
2 else
        if(day.of.year[i]>=season.intervals[5]&day.of.year[i]<=season.intervals[6]) season.var[i]<-
3 else
        if(day.of.year[i]>=season.intervals[7]&day.of.year[i]<=season.intervals[8]) season.var[i]<-
4

        }}


        #SEASONAL BOXPLOT
        windows()
        boxplot(SubData$Result.Value~season.var,xaxt='n',xlab="",ylab=paste(VarName),varwi
dth=T)

season.labels.BICA<-c("Aug. 10-Apr. 14", "Apr. 15-June 19", "June 20-Aug. 9")
season.labels.YELL<-c("Nov. 1-Apr. 15", "Apr. 16-June 15","June 16-Aug. 15","Aug. 16-Oct.
31")
season.labels.GRTE<-c("Aug. 15-April 14", "Apr. 15-June 9", "June 10-Aug. 14")

#creating labels for month

season.labels.month <-
c("Jan.","Feb.","Mar.","April","May","June","July","Aug.","Sept.","Oct.","Nov.","Dec.")

if(missing(season.location)) season.labels <- season.labels.month  else
        if(season.location=="GRTE") season.labels <- season.labels.GRTE  else
        if(season.location=="YELL") season.labels <- season.labels.YELL  else
        season.labels<-season.labels.BICA

        mtext(season.labels,side=1,at=c(1:length(season.labels)),cex=.75)

        # DISCHARGE PLOTS
```

```
        windows()
        plot(SubData$Year,SubData$Discharge..cfs.,ylim=c(0,max(SubData$Discharge)+.1),typ
e='n',xlab="Year",ylab="Discharge (cfs)")

        for(i in 1:no.season){
        points(SubData$Year[season.var==i],SubData$Discharge..cfs.[season.var==i],pch=i)
  }


if(no.season==12) legend("topleft",legend=c("Jan.","Feb.","Mar.",
"Apr.","May","Jun.","Jul.","Aug.","Sep.","Oct.","Nov.","Dec."),pch=1:12,col=1:12)  else
  if(no.season==4) legend("topleft",legend=c(" season 1","season 2","season 3", "season
4"),pch=1:4) else
  if(no.season==3) legend("topleft",legend=c(" season 1","season 2","season 3"),pch=1:3) else
print("ERROR: number of seasons wrong")


if(TEST=="noflow") OUT<-SeasonalMannKendall(SubData,season.var,no.season,VarName)
else
if(TEST=="flow") OUT<-FlowAdjust.Seasonal(SubData,season.var,no.season,VarName) else
print("Error in test option")

return(OUT)
}

        ## Kendall Functions
        power.kendall<-function(x, y){
          tau <- 0
          ptau <- 0
          sltau <- 0
    score <- 0
    varscore <- 0
    denom <- 0
    i <- !(is.na(x) | is.na(y))
    x <- x[i]
    y <- y[i]
    iws <- numeric(length(x))
    ifault <- 0
    outF <- .Fortran("tauk2", as.single(x), as.single(y), as.integer(length(x)),
       as.single(tau), as.single(ptau), as.single(sltau), as.single(score),
       as.single(varscore), as.single(denom), as.integer(iws),
       as.integer(ifault), PACKAGE = "Kendall")
    tau <- outF[[4]]
    sl <- outF[[6]]
    sc <- outF[[7]]
    var.sc <- outF[[8]]
    denom <- outF[[9]]
    ier <- outF[[11]]
    ans <- list(tau = tau, sl = sl, S = sc, D = denom, varS = var.sc)
    oldClass(ans) <- "Kendall"
    ans
```

```
        }

            power.MannKendall<-function (x) {
                power.kendall(1:length(x), x)
                }
```

SEASONAL MANN-KENDALL TEST

```
SeasonalMannKendall<-function(SubData,season.var,no.season,VarName){
        #Seasonal MannKendall TREND TESTS

        library(Kendall)

        #create function for Seasonal Mann-Kendall Test
        # THIS ASSUMES THE DATA IS IN THE SAME FORMAT AS PROVIDED IN THE FILE
        # "Soda_Butte_lower_data.csv" and then altered as above!

    # seasonal Mann-Kendall without flow test # separate data by season
        tau<-numeric()
        S<-numeric()
    n.i<-numeric()

windows()

plot(SubData$Year,SubData$Result.Value,type='n',ylab=paste(VarName,"Medians"),xlab="Yea
r",main="Seasonal Medians Across Years")

    for(k in 1:no.season){
        byseason.data<-subset(SubData,season.var==k)
                medians<-tapply(byseason.data$Result.Value,byseason.data$Year,median)
            out<-power.MannKendall(medians)
                tau[k]<-out$tau
        S[k]<-out$S
        n.i[k]<-length(medians)
    points(unique(byseason.data$Year),medians,pch=k,col=1,bg=1)
    lines(unique(byseason.data$Year),medians,lty=k)
                }
if(no.season==12) legend("topleft",legend=c("Jan.","Feb.","Mar.",
"Apr.","May","Jun.","Jul.","Aug.","Sep.","Oct.","Nov.","Dec."),pch=1:12,col=1:12)  else
if(no.season==4) legend("topleft",legend=c(" season 1","season 2","season 3", "season
4"),pch=1:4) else
   if(no.season==3) legend("topleft",legend=c(" season 1","season 2","season 3"),pch=1:3) else
print("ERROR: number of seasons wrong")

        # Calculate test statistic by summing over seasons and dividing by appropriate
sqrt(denominator)
    # See Hirsch et al. 1982 Water Resources Research Eqn. 8 and 9

            sktau<-sum(S)
            denom<-sum((n.i*(n.i-1)*(2*n.i+5)/18))
```

```r
            ts.out<-ifelse(sktau>=0,(sktau-1)/sqrt(denom),(sktau+1)/sqrt(denom))
            p.value<-1-pnorm(abs(ts.out))

if(min(n.i)<10) print("WARNING: Recommended sample size > 10")

        out<-list("S"=sktau,"Var.S"=denom,"Z-statistic"=ts.out,"P-Value"=p.value)

        return(out)

        }

#input requires the created seasonal variable, and data subset to a location, and one parameter


# FLOW ADJUSTED SEASONAL MANN-KENDALL TEST

# TEST TO ADJUST FOR FLOW FROM ALLEY (1988)
# ASSUMES NO RELATIONSHIP BETWEEN DISCHARGE AND YEAR; ALSO ASSUMES
COMMON LINEAR RELATIONSHIP BETWEEN SOLUTE AND DISCHARGE
# ACROSS SEASONS.

FlowAdjust.Seasonal<-function(in.data,season.var,no.season,VarName){
    out<-lm(in.data$Result.Value~as.factor(season.var)*in.data$Discharge..cfs.)

windows()
plot(in.data$Result.Value~in.data$Discharge..cfs.,type='n',ylim=c(min(in.data$Result.Value),ma
x(in.data$Result.Value)+.25*max(in.data$Result.Value)),
 main="Characteristic Value versus Discharge coded by
Season",ylab=paste(in.data$STORET.Characteristic.Name[1]),xlab="Discharge")
    for(i in 1:no.season){
    points(in.data$Discharge..cfs.[season.var==i],in.data$Result.Value[season.var==i],pch=i)
  }

if(no.season==12) legend("topleft",legend=c("Jan.","Feb.","Mar.",
"Apr.","May","Jun.","Jul.","Aug.","Sep.","Oct.","Nov.","Dec."),pch=1:12,col=1:12)  else
if(no.season==4) legend("topleft",legend=c(" season 1","season 2","season 3", "season
4"),pch=1:4) else
   if(no.season==3) legend("topleft",legend=c(" season 1","season 2","season 3"),pch=1:3) else
print("ERROR: number of seasons wrong")


 flow.adj<-data.frame(out$res,in.data$Year)
   names(flow.adj)<-c("Result.Value","Year")

print("WARNING: THIS FUNCTION ASSUMES THERE IS LINEAR RELATIONSHIP BETWEEN
CHARACTERISTIC VALUE AND DISCHARGE")
print("WARNING: THIS FUNCTION ASSUMES THERE IS NO YEARLY TREND IN
DISCHARGE")
        OUT<-SeasonalMannKendall(flow.adj,season.var,no.season,VarName)
        return(OUT)
}
```

Appendix E: Step-by-Step Guide to Running the Trend Analysis R Code and the Generated Output

Step 1. Manipulate data from NPStoret

1) A JulianDate field (column) needs to be added. This was accomplished using the following formula in Excel **=RIGHT(YEAR(A1),2)&TEXT(A1-DATE(YEAR(A1),1,0),"000")**. This converts a date in cell A1 to a Julian Date. This formula is from the website http://www.cpearson.com/excel/jdates.htm . The website description is "This formula takes the 2 right-most characters of the YEAR of the date in A1, and then appends the number of days between the date in A1 and the 0th day of that year. The TEXT function formats the day-of-year number as three digits, with leading zeros if necessary."

2) For the R-code to run, the column headings need to be the same as the file used to build the script (see Table 2.1). Verify this is true.

3) Create a separate column for month, day, and year from the "Visit Start Date" column. We used the text to column option under the Data tab in excel with '/' as the separator.

4) The Excel file should be saved as a comma delimited file with extension .csv.

Step 2. Import data into R

data.test<-read.csv("Soda_Butte_lower_data.csv")

Step 3. Submit all commands in file "GRYN_Trend_Functions_March2012.R"

Make sure script is "active" in R, then go to pull down Edit menu (located on toolbar)— select run all.

Step 4. Install R package Kendall, instructions can be found in Appendix F.

Step 5. Running the code, commands in file "GRYN_ExampleTrendCommands_March2012.R"

The following sulfate example shows an analysis with and without flow weighting for 4 seasons based on the hydrograph for Yellowstone. Another option is to specify the season as month as with the power analysis comparison. For this option the season.location should be missing and the no.season should be 12. The command follows,

GRYN.TREND.WATER(data.input=data.test,VarName="Sulfate",no.season=12,TEST="noflow")

Sulfate Example
Option 1. No flow adjustment (Seasonal Mann-Kendall test for trend)
Option 1: Run function without flow adjustment

GRYN.TREND.WATER(data.input=data.test,VarName="Sulfate",season.location="YELL",no.season=4,TEST="noflow")

Output:

1] "WARNING: Recommended sample size > 10"

$S

[1] 4

$Var.S

[1] 14.66667

$`Z-statistic`

[1] 0.7833495

$`P-Value`

[1] 0.2167110

The warning message is to alert the user that less than 10 years are available for analysis. S is the value of the seasonal Mann-Kendall statistic (in this example, S = 4). Var.S is the variance of the statistic (Var.S=14.66667). Z-statistic is the value used to compare to the standard normal distribution to find the p-value. The calculation is based on Equations 8 (Var.S) and 9 (Z-statistic) in Hirsch et al. (1982) and the text first column page 110 (S).

The following plots are automatically generated:

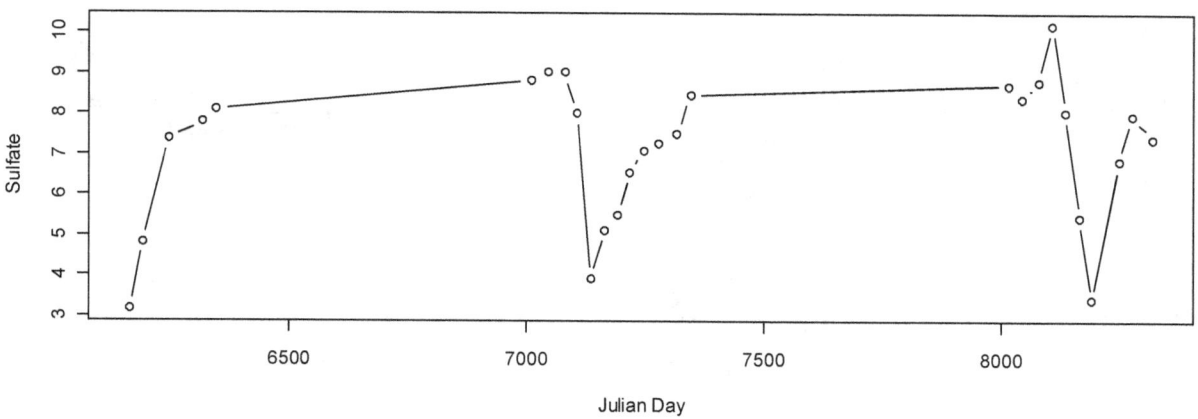

Figure E1. The characteristic values versus Julian Day. This is a time series plot of the actual result values.

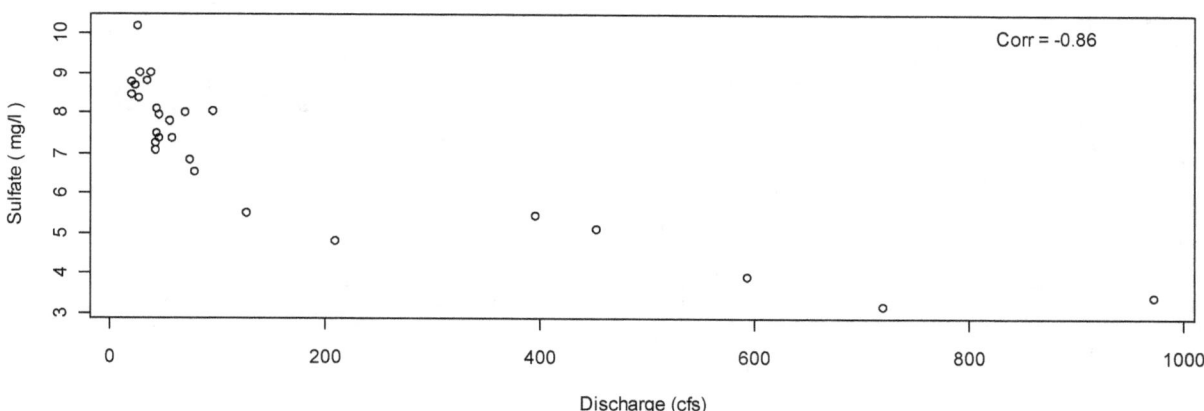

Figure E2. Characteristic versus discharge. Notice for sulfate there is evidence of a negative correlation between sulfate (mg/L) and discharge, suggesting the appropriate analysis is to adjust for flow.

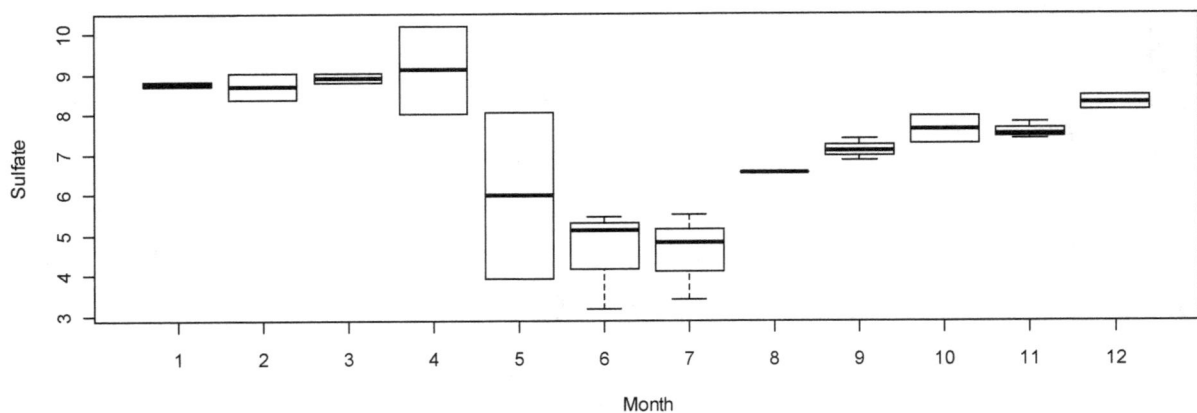

Figure E3. Monthly boxplots of characteristic of interest

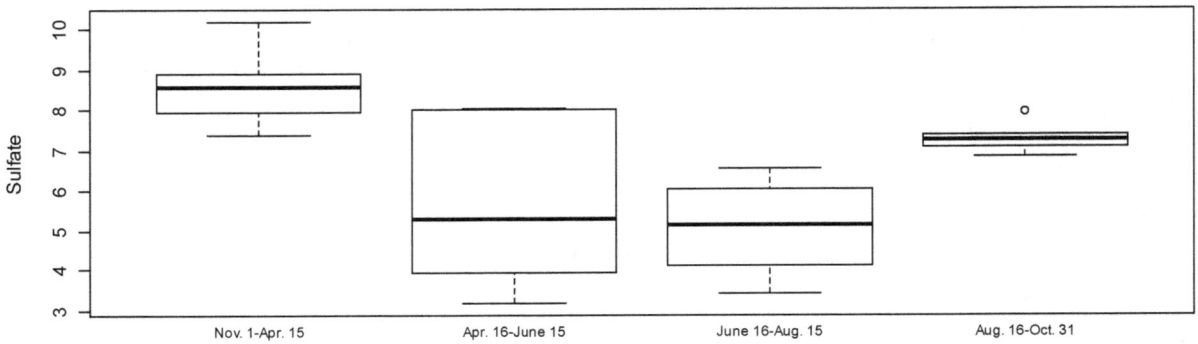

Figure E4. Seasonal boxplot of characteristic of interest.

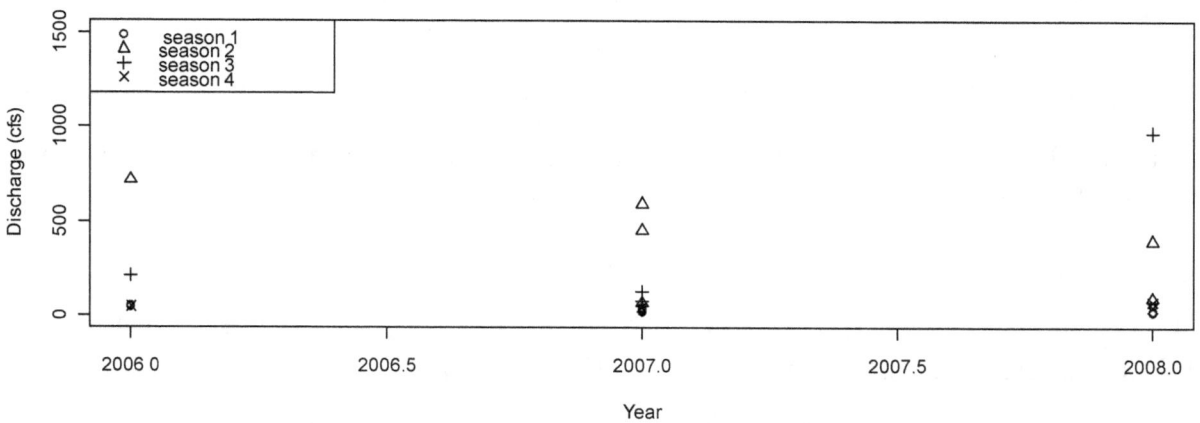

Figure E5. Discharge versus year by season. To assess whether there is evidence of a trend in discharge over time.

Seasonal Medians Across Years

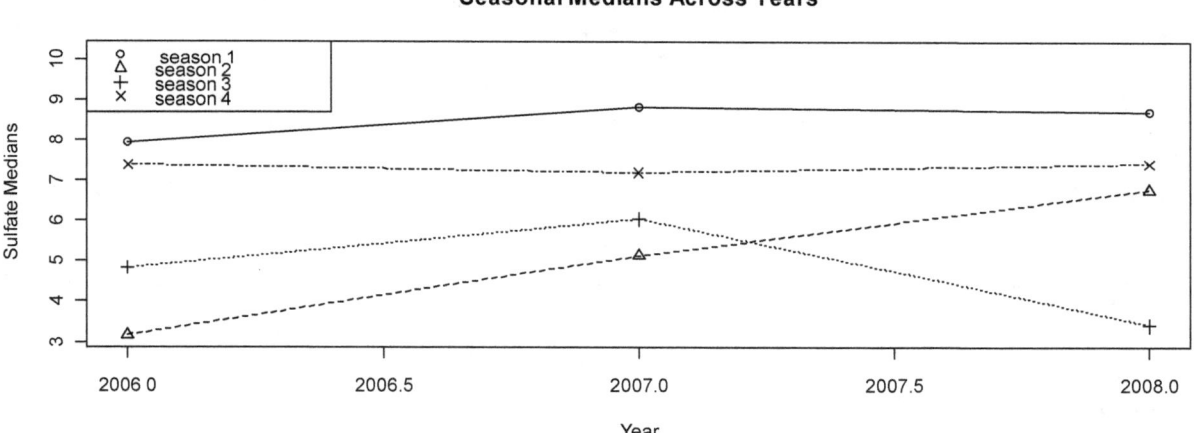

Figure E6. Seasonal medians of sulfate over years by season. This is the data used in the seasonal Mann-Kendall test without flow adjustment. Notice if the p-value is non-significant this plot can verify whether it is due to seasons having opposite patterns (increasing and decreasing over years) as opposed to the same pattern for all seasons across years.

Option 2. Flow Adjusted analysis (Seasonal Mann-Kendall test for trend on residuals)
Based on Figure 2.2, one should consider flow adjustment for sulfate. The following R command does that:

Option 2: Run function with flow adjustment

GRYN.TREND.WATER(data.input=data.test,VarName="Sulfate",season.location="YELL",no.season=4,TEST="flow")

Output:

1] "WARNING: THIS FUNCTION ASSUMES THERE IS LINEAR RELATIONSHIP BETWEEN CHARACTERISTIC VALUE AND DISCHARGE"

[1] "WARNING: THIS FUNCTION ASSUMES THERE IS NO YEARLY TREND IN DISCHARGE"

[1] "WARNING: Recommended sample size > 10"

$S

[1] 0

$Var.S

[1] 14.66667

$`Z-statistic`

[1] -0.2611165

$`P-Value`

[1] 0.3970013

There are several warning messages included in the R function because of our concern over the potential misuse of a p-value without considering whether the assumptions are met for the test to be valid. Alley (1988) lays out the framework for when this approach should be used. A simple linear regression of characteristic on discharge was significant at the 0.05 level. IF there is a significant relationship between year and discharge, a different approach should be used. Also, the code adjusted for discharge within each season. Note the results change if we assume the same relationship between discharge and sulfate across seasons. The following output graphics assist with deciding if this is the appropriate test to use.

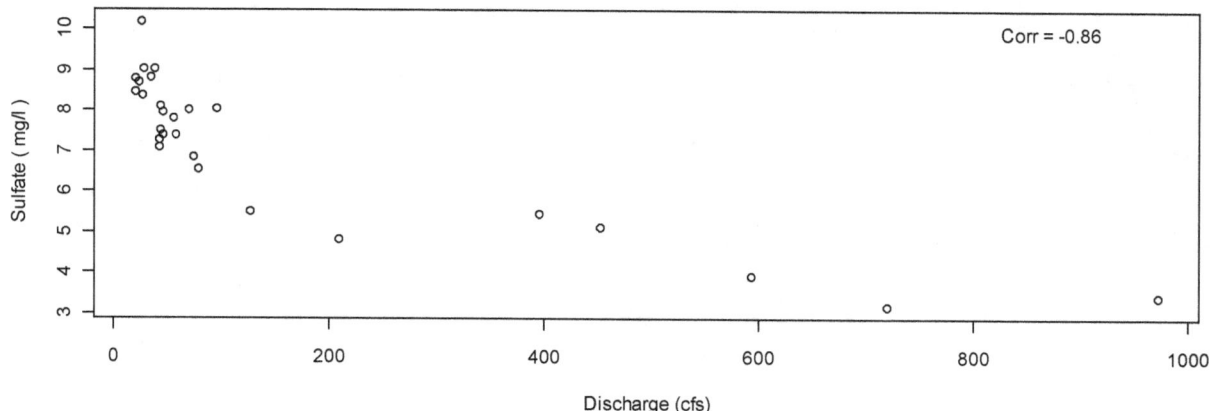

Figure E7. Sulfate versus discharge.

Shows there is a relationship between discharge and sulfate, with correlation = -0.86.

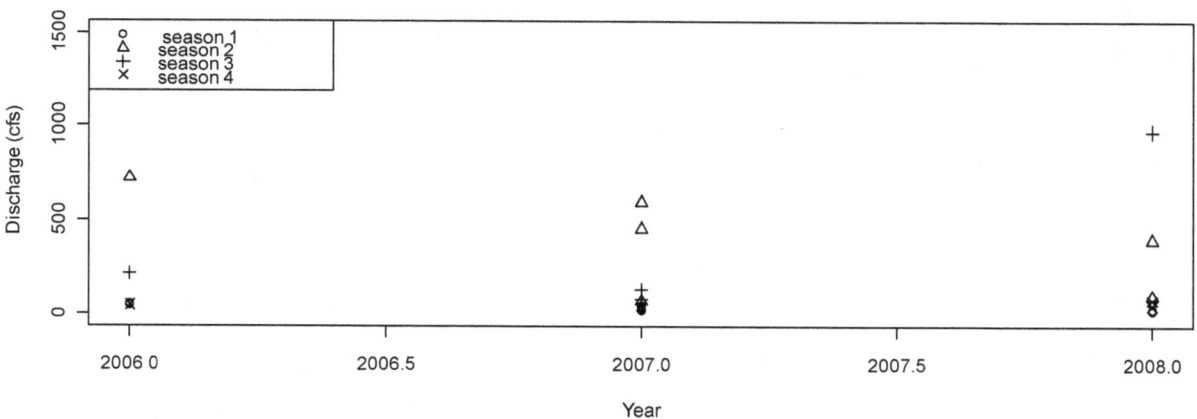

Figure E8. Discharge coded by season across years. This plot can be used to assess whether there is evidence of a trend in discharge. Based on this plot, there doesn't appear to be one.

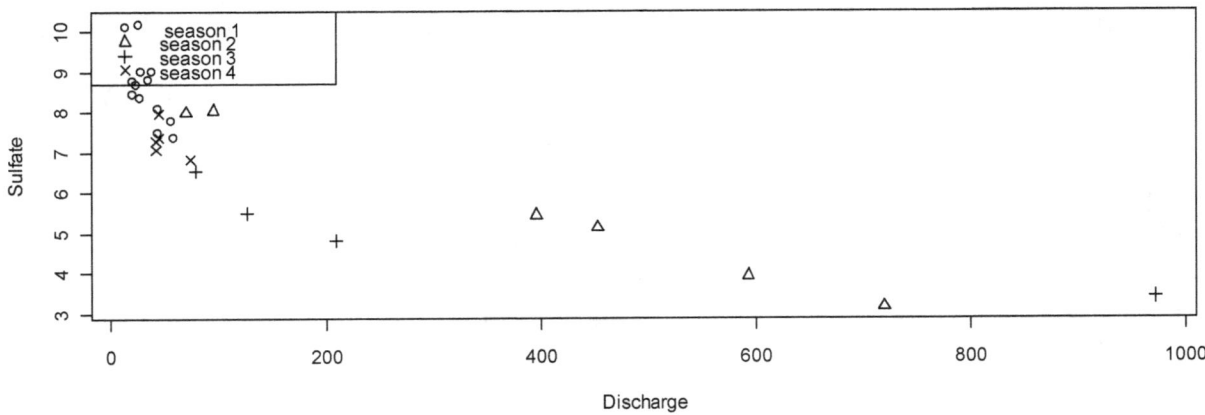

Figure E9. Sulfate versus discharge coded by season. This plot can be used to assess whether there is evidence that the relationship is the same or different across seasons. In this case, it seems there is a difference across seasons.

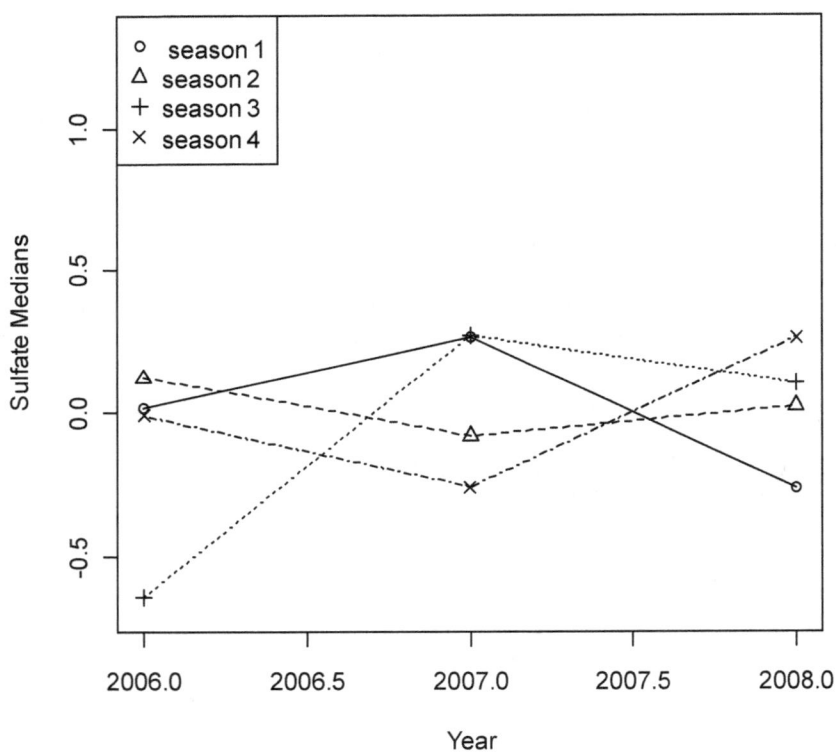

Figure E10. Sulfate medians adjusted for discharge across years by season. Notice this figure compared to Figure F6, shows that adjusting for discharge changes the pattern across seasons.

Again, a key assumption is that there is no trend in discharge across years.

Appendix F: Installing a Package in R

Step 1. Select Install package(s) from the Packages pull down menu.

Packages → Install package(s)

Step 2. Select a CRAN mirror (usually the most proximal, countries are listed alphabetically), and click OK.

Step 3. Select the package(s) you wish to upload (for this analysis you will install Kendall), and click OK.

NPS 960/115849, July 2012